Yes, You Really Can

Yes, You Really Can

Live the Life of Your Dreams

CARLA BURROWS

iUniverse, Inc.
New York   Bloomington

Yes, You Really Can
Live the Life of Your Dreams

iUniverse books may be ordered through booksellers or by contacting:

iUniverse
1663 Liberty Drive
Bloomington, IN 47403
www.iuniverse.com
1-800-Authors (1-800-288-4677)

ISBN: 978-1-4502-3565-5 (sc)
ISBN: 978-1-4502-3566-2 (ebook)

Printed in the United States of America

iUniverse rev. date: 6/15/2010

All scripture quotations, unless otherwise indicated are taken from
the Holy Bible, New International Version®, Copyright © 1973,
1978, 1984 by International Bible Society. Scripture quotations
marked (KJV) are from The King James Version of the Bible

This book is dedicated to the memories of my sister, Odessa Conyers-Simone, my grandmother, Florine Williamson, and my niece Tahoney. You will always be remembered.

Contents

Acknowledgments   ix

Introduction   xi

Who Are You, Really?   1

Your Abundant Life   7

A Guide Shall Lead the Way   13

Something New   18

Extra! Extra! Read All About It   23

It's All in Your Mind   29

Get in the Game   34

Trying Times   39

Where Are You?   44

It's All about You   50

A New Life Attitude   55

Maintain Your Strength   60

Consider Your Ways   64

Your Gifts Will Open Doors   69

Express Yourself   73

Stay on the Path   77

Say Good-bye   82

It's Not Really about You!   86

Fear is Not an Option   90

Take the First Step   94

Joy, Joy, Joy   98

The Truth of the Matter   102

Delight in His Will   106

Embrace Your Uniqueness   111

Doing Things God's Way   115

Wait On   119

Live Your Dreams out Loud   124

Big is Just an Illusion 128
The Way Is Made Known 134
The Other Side of the Storm 139
Yes, You Really Can 145
Do Something 150
About the Author 157

Acknowledgments

I would like to thank the center of my life—my Lord, my God. Without him, nothing is possible, but through him, all things really are possible.

I would like to thank my family, Mom Odessa, sisters Quincy and Tonya, my brothers, Greg, Lamonse, and Leon, and my brother-in-laws, Eddie and Reggie. I see the gift of God in each of you. Each one of you inspires me in your own unique way.

I would like to thank all my nieces and nephews and my extended family— too numerous to name. You each give me a reason to keep striving to be all that I can be, with the hope that I will somehow inspire each one of you to pursue Christ and God's purpose for your life.

I would like to thank my spiritual family, Pastor James and Linda Clarke, Assistant Pastor David and Rebecca Jones, and the entire Power of Praise Church family, located in Hopewell, VA. You were God's gift to me at one of the most critical times in my life. I could not have handpicked a more wonderful spiritual family.

A thanks to my special friends—Angel Mikell, Michelle Wilson, Carolyn Jones, Faye Hughes, Tonika Clarke-Tuppince, and Torasha Armstrong, thank you for all your prayers and support over the years.

To Mr. Tyson and everyone else who has ever believed in and supported me, I thank you.

Most of all, I would like to thank my husband, Terry. You have become my greatest support. Thank you for believing in me.

Introduction

Congratulations on your decision to live the life of your dreams. I believe that every one of God's children has a dream in his or her heart. For some of you, those dreams seem impossible. *Yes, You Really Can* is an invitation to all believers to start living the life of your dreams today. Whether you want to fulfill a lifelong dream or discover and live your life's purpose, *Yes, You Really Can* is the inspiration you need to guide you on your path to success.

Like many people who sense a calling to something greater in their lives, I made a firm decision to overcome fears, doubts, and self-limiting beliefs that were holding me back from following my heart's desires. My journey has led me to discover my authentic purpose and start living the life of my dreams.

I am so excited that you have this book in your hand right now. I believe with all of my heart that we have connected for a reason. I wrote this book with you in mind; a motivated, hope-filled believer, who knows that there is a unique purpose for your life and long to discover and create the life of your dreams.

I will show you how to break free from your own fears, doubts, and self-limiting beliefs, which are holding you back from living the life you deserve and desire.

This book of practical wisdom will inspire you to take the steps to:

- discover who you really are;
- listen to your spirit and get clarity for your life;
- overcome fears, doubts, and self-limiting beliefs;
- discover your authentic purpose;
- stop dreaming and start living your abundant life;
- create a strategic plan for your inspired dreams;
- persevere through the storms in your life.

I have included exercises, a focus thought and my very own coaching challenge at the end of each chapter.

I've also included a journal that you can use to record your thoughts, prayer, or anything that you discover about yourself or your dreams along the way.

I sincerely hope that reading this book will awaken a realization within you that *Yes, You Really Can* live the life of your dreams.

Who Are You, Really?

Then God said, "Let us make man in our own image,
in our likeness."
                                        —Genesis 1:26

I have spent most of my life in search of myself. I was always
trying to figure out exactly who I was. *Who am I, really,* I used
to wonder. There was some comfort in knowing that I shared
a bond with my six siblings. There was even more comfort in
noticing the resemblance between my mom and myself. None
of that, however, satisfied my curiosity about who I was as an
individual. Because of this uncertainty, I was always in search
of something or someone with which I could identify.

Occasionally I would encounter someone who "got" me,
someone who understood my quirkiness. Now and again
someone would come along and find my dry sense of humor
and quiet nature refreshing. Others, however, would find those
very things intimidating. There were times when I felt that
people just did not find me interesting or fun to be around.
Eventually I came to realize that I could not look to other people
to define who I was or to give my life value and meaning.

In my quest to find my authentic self, there was only one
logical place to look: I had to turn to the one person I could

trust to be totally honest and real with me—the one person who knew more about me than my own mother did—and that person was God.

In your search to discover who you really are, there is only one place to start. You will find that you are fashioned in the reflection and likeness of God, sharing his amazing distinctiveness. "In the beginning," as the Bible says, when God began the creation process, around him was nothing, and darkness was everywhere. Nevertheless, God in his splendor had the unique ability to breathe life into whatever he chose and create something good out of darkness and emptiness.

When God created man, he did not look outside himself, nor did he look for a flamboyant object. He took something as simple as dust from the earth, something with no real significance, and breathed life into it. He gave from within himself that he might add life to his creation, and afterward, God blessed it.

Your blessings include the ability to re-create the life that you live. You, created in God's image, have the ability to create something from emptiness. God breathed into you unique abilities, talents, and gifts. He breathed into you the ability to do and become whatever you choose.

In order to live the authentic and abundant life you deserve and desire, you must first become aware of what is inside you. You must first become aware of the inner person, the true person. We see the physical body, but I challenge you to get to know the self that feels, that desires, and longs for things unknown: the self beneath the one that hides from our truths and looks for material objects to hide our nakedness; the person underneath the one that adorns himself or herself with apparel in an attempt to cover up our imperfections, hidden agendas, hurts, disappointments, and shame.

Awareness is about awakening to the inner truth of who God created you to be. It is about fully understanding what you are capable of creating and achieving in your life. The moment you become aware of this sacred truth, the easier and faster it will become to create and live the life of your dreams.

Before you can grasp the reality of who you really are, you must come to understand that the person you appear to be is just a perception built around the many roles you have attached yourself to throughout your life.

Other people often play an influential part in our identities by telling us who they think we are or by advising us on who they feel we should or should not become. They may even at times suggest what we can or cannot accomplish in life. These bold opinions of others strongly influence how we sometimes perceive ourselves and limit our ability to believe in our dreams.

Understanding who you really are will enlighten you about your unique gifts, talents, and skills. It will reveal to you how to overcome challenges in life. Knowing who you are will bring you to a clearer understanding of what matters to you, your purpose in life. This awareness allows you to acknowledge your weaknesses and strengths. It identifies hidden agendas that exist and any area in need of healing. You will begin to get a better understanding of the paths you are to travel in your life. Get to know God and gain insight about the authentic you.

Take the First Step

Spend quiet time meditating on these scriptures:
- 1 John 4:4
- Philippians 4:13
- Romans 8:17
- 1 Peter 2:9
- 2 Timothy 1:7

1. After meditating on the above scripture, what truth resonated with you?

_____

_____

_____

_____

_____

_____

_____

2. What is it that you desire to create in your life? Take a moment to list the top five things you want for your life.

_____

_____

_____

_____

_____

_____

_____

3. Write out at least three positive affirmations about the person you really are or the life you desire to create.

_____

_____

_____

_____

_____

_____

_____

Focused Thought:

"Look to the one who created you to discover who you really are."

Carla's Coaching Challenge

Make a decision today to look within, at the person God created you to be, so that you can discover who you really are. Stop allowing others' perceptions of you determine the life that you live. Take some time out to identify what false truths you have believed in the past. Write out at least three new truths that you have discovered about yourself.

Journal Entry

Your Abundant Life

For as he thinketh in his heart, so is he.
>   —Proverbs 23:7 (KJV)

I used to create visions for my life based on my necessities. I would only allow myself to create a life that provided security and stability. There is nothing wrong with that, other than the fact that I never really followed my heart. I would listen to the thoughts in my head, the thoughts that informed me that I had to choose the safe, responsible, secure way. I believed that this was the only way that would provide provision for my future. Real vision, I have come to understand, begins in the heart.

You must learn to tune out the thoughts in your head as you began to write out your visions. Your head will tell you what you can do within reason and give you every reason why you cannot accomplish what is in your heart. God's word states, however, that we are the very thoughts of our heart. Your heartfelt passions will lead you into living the abundant life you have desired, if you keep these thoughts at the forefront of your daily meditations. Whatever you are passionate about will bring about your abundant lifestyle, if you allow yourself to focus on these thoughts.

Jesus came to earth so that we can have full lives—lives of abundance and joy. In order to live that full life, you need to determine what that is for you. Search your heart; take time to meditate and ask yourself what really matters to you. If you could really live the life of your dreams, what would it look like? There are no boundaries in visions; there are no limits to the extent that you can dream. It is whatever you feel and sense in your heart.

Do you imagine yourself living in a four-bedroom home overlooking a lake, or does your home have a beautiful rose garden, surrounded by lots of greenery? Maybe your heart is set on living in the middle of a downtown district with lots of gourmet restaurants, antique shops, boutiques, and outdoor cafés. Perhaps your heart longs to help abandoned children find caring families. You may have been born with a supportive family that loves and supports you, and the thought of a young child alone in the world could be the very thing that ignites you to make a difference. Maybe you have a passion to mentor young girls who have endured abuse because you yourself endured the same, and you understand how devastating it can be to live a life feeling unsafe and walking through life with self-doubt and low self-esteem.

No one else can give you your vision; you have to search your heart and then transfer that vision to your thoughts. Get a vision in your mind, starting with who you are as a person. Search your heart to find out what you desire for every area of your life. Include every aspect, such as financial, physical, spiritual, family, career, community, and recreation. Think about your heart's desires as often as you can throughout the day and begin to live the abundant life you deserve and desire.

Take the First Step

1. Plan time alone in your favorite quiet spot and search your heart. It could be lounging in your

favorite chair, sitting under a big oak tree in the park, soaking in a tub full of bubbles, or taking a walk. After you are done, describe in detail your heartfelt desires.

_____

_____

_____

_____

_____

_____

_____

2. Imagine what it feels like to live out your dream.

_____

_____

_____

_____

_____

_____

_____

3. Describe your ideal life in each area listed below.

Financial

_____

_____

_____

_____

Physical/Health

_____

_____

_____
_____
_____

Spiritual

_____
_____
_____
_____

Career/Education

_____
_____
_____
_____

Family/Relationships

_____
_____
_____
_____

Fun

_____
_____
_____
_____
_____

Charity/Community

_____

_____

_____

_____

_____

_____

Focused Thought:

"Focus your thoughts on your heartfelt desires and passion."

Carla's Coaching Challenge

Dare to stop creating a vision for your life from a place of lack or need. I am not saying not to make some decision to take care of your current situation; I do encourage you, however, to challenge yourself to dream of a future based simply on the desires of your heart.

Journal Entry

A Guide Shall Lead the Way

Whether you turn to the right or to the left, your ears will hear a voice behind you saying, "This is the way: walk in it."

—Isaiah 30:21

A crossroads has more than one pathway; choosing the right one will get you to *your* destination. There are times when we find ourselves in unfamiliar territories, in an unfamiliar place. When this happens, we usually become anxious and sometimes fearful. It is during these times that we wish we had some type of a roadmap—a GPS system or navigator. Some type of guide that would get us back on the right road, headed in the direction of our original destination.

I remember a specific time in my life when I found myself on a path that in time would have led to a place of darkness and ruin. I was not making the right decisions for my life. I knew that I wanted a change, but my friends and my lifestyle were the strongest influence in my life at that time. One could say I was lost. Nonetheless, I felt at home in that place at that time in my life.

One night during this particular time of my life, I heard a strong voice that said to me, "No more." The voice that I heard came from inside me. The words were short and to the point, and I needed no further explanation. This was the voice of God speaking to me as a father would to one of his precious children.

That voice once again became my saving grace and directed me back onto the path of life—a path of safety, a place of hope, and a beautiful future.

In life you will find yourself at many crossroads, and it is during this time that you will realize that you are equipped with a built-in navigator—your own personal guide. As you are standing at a crossroads, you will hear your guide telling you which direction to take in life—the direction that will lead you to your ultimate destination.

Everyone has a unique path to follow. Once you have decided what you want out of life and make the decision to move forward to obtain all that you desire, other people will either get excited and begin to offer their advice on what you should do, or they will be against you and suggest that you take another route. You will hear about great opportunities that may be of interest to you, things that may or may not assist you in reaching your destination. You will hear of alternate paths to take that can get you close to where you want to go but that do not allow you the privilege of doing what you are passionate about.

Become familiar with the voice you hear behind your ear. This is the central voice to trust when making life's choices; walk in the direction of that voice. Sometimes that voice will concur with the advice from others; only then should you listen to and follow their guidance.

If you find yourself moving on a whim because this is what others around you are doing, knowing full well that it is not in alignment with your own true desires or beliefs, then you are wasting valuable time. You are no longer being true to yourself, and you are no longer living your authentic life. I am not trying to say that you should not allow someone of experience, wisdom, and knowledge to lead and guide you along your path; what I am suggesting is that you pray and ask God to send the right people, at the right time. These chosen people will be instrumental in assisting you in fulfilling your purpose in life. When they show up, a voice within you will let you know that they are to council you at that time.

God has placed within each of us a personal guide; because of this, we are extremely blessed. Your personal guide will lead you and direct you throughout life. Refusing to listen to this voice will lead you down paths unknown. You have no need to get anxious when you come to the crossroads of your life; all you need to do is listen to that still, quiet voice within you. You will never truly be lost or without direction as long as you are obedient to the voice of God directing you.

Take the First Step

1. Are you standing at a crossroads in your life right now? What decisions do you need to consider?

_____

_____

_____

_____

_____

_____

_____

_____

2. Familiarize yourself with that voice guiding you. In the space below, state how you identify that voice. Is it a feeling, an instinct, or a small, quiet voice?

_____

_____

_____

_____

_____

_____

_____

_____

3. Have you discovered any special direction for your
   life recently? If so, write it out in the space below.

_____

_____

_____

_____

_____

_____

_____

Focused Thought:

"Listen to the voice of your spirit."

Carla's Coaching Challenge

Spend a set amount of time daily simply listening. Find a quiet
place where you will not be disturbed. Focus on a beautiful
object or place. Start out with five minutes daily. When you are
finished, record your thoughts.

Journal Entry

Something New

See, I am doing a new thing! Now it springs up; do you not perceive it?

—Isaiah 43:19

As I have mentioned before, true desires are born in the heart. Have you ever found yourself longing for something, but you are not sure what it was? The only thing that you know for sure is that your intuition is telling you that something new is about to happen. It is that feeling you get deep within, that longing for a more satisfying life, that feeling that never seems to go away. The truth of the matter is that God is trying to move you in a new direction, into paths not yet traveled, to a place that will give your life meaning and fulfill the desires of your heart.

Once those feelings start nagging at your heart, you must take the time necessary to understand why. Sometimes it is a signal that you have gotten off the path designed for you and God is saying to you, "Today is a new day, a new opportunity to live your heart's desires." Maybe your dreams have been on hold so that you could raise your children, support your mate's dream, or take care of a sick loved one. It could even be that you have spent most of your life in survival mode, unable to consider dreaming past making it through another day. Sometimes life can be one struggle after another, full of letdowns and disappointments. God is saying, "That was then; this is now." That inkling in your heart is leading you to believe that your time is now.

Stretch your mind to anticipate something great happening in your life. God desires to do something for you that you have never experienced before. Maybe even something that no one else in your family has ever experienced. You may feel a nudge from your spirit to pursue a master's degree. Maybe you will be the first entrepreneur or millionaire in your family. You may be praying for enough income to support your immediate family; God may be saying to you, however, "What I have in store for you is enough not only for your family but enough to benefit multiple families in your community with more than enough left over to impact generations to come."

Take the time necessary to figure out what your heart is longing for. Surrender to the way of your heart; be willing to allow God to do something new in your life. To ignore this feeling is to miss the opportunity to live your abundant life. Feel the anticipation in your spirit. You may find yourself fearful of doing something completely new or becoming a person you never dreamed you could be, but have faith that God knows what he is doing. Be willing to go in a new direction, and get ready to live the life you deserve and desire.

Take the First Step

What has God been trying to reveal to you lately? Have you been feeling as if you should try something new or do something out of the ordinary?

1. In the space below, identify any new direction or new opportunity you feel led to pursue.

_____

_____

_____

_____

_____

_____

_____

_____

2. Identify one step you can take today to start walking in this newness of your life.

_____

_____

_____

_____

_____

_____

_____

_____

3. Are you encountering any fears that may interfere with God's plans for your life? If so, write them out here.

_____

_____

_____

_____

_____

_____

_____

_____

Focused Thought:

"If you find yourself daydreaming about doing something that you have not done before or going somewhere you have never been, it could mean that God is calling you to a new direction."

Carla's Coaching Challenge

Play the "what if" game. The next time you find yourself thinking about doing something new, ask yourself "What if?" For example:

Ask yourself: what would happen if I took the new job and got a better position and an increase in pay? What if I went back to school and got a great job paying double my salary? What if I started my own business and it became a success in one year? What if I started exercising thirty minutes a day and ended up losing twenty pounds? What if I followed my heart, moved to another city, met many new friends, and lived in a great neighborhood? What if I gave up this bad habit, and my whole life changed in a positive way? What if I trusted God and ended up influencing the lives of others in a great way?

Try this with every new thought that comes to you. Imagine that what God is trying to show you is a brighter future.

Journal Entry

Extra! Extra! Read All About It

Then the Lord replied: "Write down the revelation and make it plain on tablets so that a herald may run with it."

—Habakkuk 2:2

The visionary is the only one who can design a detailed and accurate blueprint. Remember that you are the center of your life's design. You get the opportunity to write your own story. No one has the ability to write your part the way you can because you are the only one with all the unique details. Yours is the only heart that is able to get a true picture of how the story goes.

Have you ever found yourself sitting or standing at work, looking around, wondering what in the world were you doing in that place? On a couple of occasions in the past, I have found myself wondering whose life I was living—certainly not the one I had envisioned for myself.

On one occasion in particular, I was at work. It was another fast-paced, stressful day. I was enjoying the part of my job that consisted of encouraging and offering hope to my clients and their families. I was also enjoying the everyday interactions with my co-workers. In that moment, however, I had an epiphany. I stood still in my tracks and thought to myself, *this is not what I signed up to do.* I was running here and there, doing too much, too fast, without even a moment to seek God's guidance about decisions I needed to make or time to collect my thoughts. It dawned on me at that very moment that I was not in harmony with my dreams or my values, or—in particular—with God's will for my life. I had to refocus and seek God for direction.

Eventually, I set out to find a job that was in line with my values, talents, and needs.

Have you ever found yourself wondering whose life you are living? If so, you need to reconsider exactly what it is you want for your life. Once you have thought long and hard about your desires and needs, write it down, make it plain, and do not leave anything out.

What type of work do you see yourself doing? What position can you imagine yourself occupying? Are you in a downtown office suite? Are you a landscape architect or an entrepreneur? Write it down. Do you earn in the thousands, do you have a six-figure salary, or does your dream require that you make no less than several million? It could be that you see yourself as a volunteer in a nonprofit agency. Write it all down. How many kids do you see in your life? What type of car do you drive? What type of personality does your mate exhibit?

Write it all down. Details do matter, and if you are not specific about what you want for your life you may end up with some of the qualities or details you desire, however you may also end up with a few things that you could never in a million years have pictured in your mind. Write down everything you can imagine. Your vision is just that—yours.

I remember a couple of years ago, while attending a class, working toward a business degree, my assignment was to write a business plan. I decided to write out a plan for a vision that God had given me a year or so prior. From the moment I glimpsed this vision, I had a desire in my heart to start a business geared toward women, empowering them in every area of their lives. I gave a copy of that business plan to my instructor for a grade, but I also gave a copy to my pastor and one of my dearest friends so that they could pray with me concerning the vision. At that time, it appeared to be a far-fetched vision, just a dream downloaded into my heart. A few months later, I received a certification to teach women's seminars, I obtained a license for my business, and I started taking a course to receive a certification as a life coach. Later I coauthored a book entitled "A Woman's Handbook For Self-Confidence." Now I am writing this book with plans to self-publish. Even though writing the book was not in my business plan, it was a part of my vision—the part that I thought was a far-fetched dream that belonged to someone else. Nevertheless, it was always tugging at the back of my mind. Also, I have given up the notion of business college; it was never in my vision to balance debits and credits, neither for others nor for myself.

This is just a reminder that following biblical principles will lead you to success. Write out your vision, and be clear about what you desire. Share your vision with others who believe in you and your abilities, with people who believe in the God that is able to do all things.

Take the First Step

1. Take a few minutes right now to write down your No. 1 vision. Whether written as a journal entry, on the computer, or as a full business plan, just write it.

_____

_____

_____

_____

_____

_____

_____

2. With whom can you share your vision? Whom can you trust to support you and pray for your success?

_____

_____

_____

_____

_____

_____

_____

_____

_____

3. Rewrite your vision in one sentence in the space below.

_____

_____

_____

_____

_____

_____

_____

Focused Thought:

Writing out your vision makes it more real and allows you to put it in a place where you can read it daily to remind yourself of your purpose.

Carla's Coaching Challenge

Put some real thought into what you want for your life. Write
out your goals and a plan of action for accomplishing them.

Journal Entry

It's All in Your Mind

Do not conform any longer to the pattern of this world, but be transformed by the renewing of your mind. Then you will be able to test and approve what God's will is.

—Romans 12:2

You have the power within you to draw into your life all that God desires for you by meditation on spiritual principles and promises. You have the power to become the person and live the lifestyle that is yours for the asking by accepting the will of God for your life. You must no longer focus on your past behaviors, lifestyle, or negative attitude. Neither should you focus on anyone who is opposed to your resolution to change; rather, you should become the person you have made the decision to become.

Your thoughts of your life must be congruent with the thoughts of God concerning you. Your daily thoughts must always be in line with the decisions and goals you have made for yourself. The thoughts that you allow to penetrate and take up residence in your mind will ultimately determine the lifestyle that you live. There will be occasions when negative thoughts will pop up in your head unexpectedly; you have a choice, however, as to whether you entertain these thoughts or expel them from your mind by replacing them with God's truths. Make a firm decision not to allow other people or your past circumstances to determine your future.

I have talked with countless people who refused to have a conversation about a brighter future, much less dream about a brighter future for themselves. Many are not open to trying, even for a minute second; this is obvious from their conversations, which focus on the negative circumstances of their past and present. For example, I was having a conversation with an acquaintance of mine who started talking about her desire to have a home of her own. I began telling her how she could take the step to make her dream a reality, but she did not want to discuss it any further. She proceeded to tell me all the reasons why she could not afford to purchase a home. Her facial expressions showed doubt in her willingness to consider the idea. Her statement to me was, "If it is God's will, it will happen on its own." I know firsthand that there are many things that I cannot accomplish by my ability alone, but Philippians 4:13 reminds me that "I can do all things through Christ who strengthens me."

Our lives and circumstances change when we renew our thoughts. You cannot move forward toward a brighter future by focusing on the past. Think about a credit card that has expired. As hard as you might try to purchase a new item with the expired card, the outcome will be a statement that says something like "transaction failed." It is the same when you try to move forward toward an abundant life. If you continue to allow thoughts of past failures, mistakes, lost relationships, disappointments, and rejections to stay at the forefront of your mind and penetrate your heart, the outcome will always be "failure." Unless you change the negative thought patterns, this will continue be the way you see yourself and your circumstances.

Just as the credit card company will send a new card to replace the expired one and will allow your transactions to go through successfully, you will have success in life if you renew your mind by getting rid of negative thought patterns and replacing them with new, positive thoughts of a brighter future.

What you focus on throughout the day has a huge influence on what direction you will travel. Remember that your thoughts today determine where you will be tomorrow. Living the life of your dreams is possible if you choose to focus on achieving your goals. Determine your own future, and trust that God will always be with you, guiding you.

Take the First Step

1. Make a list of any negative thoughts that seem to creep up whenever you focus on living your dreams.

_____

_____

_____

_____

_____

_____

_____

2. For every negative thought above, write out a positive thought.

_____

_____

_____

_____

_____

_____

_____

3. Make a list of positive affirmations that you can focus on so that you can immediately replace the negative thought listed above.

_____

_____

_____

_____

_____

_____

_____

_____

_____

Focused Thought:

"Refuse to dwell on any negative thoughts that are out of alignment with your dreams."

Carla's Coaching Challenge

Remember to focus on things that are in line with your visions and goals. Meditate on scriptures that tell you of God's promises for your life.

Journal Entry

_____

_____

_____

_____

_____

_____

_____

_____

_____

_____

_____

_____

_____

_____

_____

_____

_____

_____

_____

_____

_____

_____

_____

_____

_____

_____

_____

_____

_____

_____

Get in the Game

Let us run with perseverance the race marked out for us.

Hebrews 12:1

Before marathon runners can participate in a race, they must first sign up for the game, making a commitment to finish the race. Once committed, they must show up at the set time with every intention to run. Whether there is rain, snow, sleet, or blazing heat, they must show up focused on the task.

I used to dream of having my own office one day—not an office that belonged to my employer, but my own office, one that represented me as a self-employed individual. I knew that it would probably happen one day in the distant future. I decided, however, that I did not want to wait. I could have my own office now. I did not have to wait until I was self-employed or until I was able to start my own business. I could create my own office right in my own home. I could fix it up any way that I desired and start working for myself on a part-time base while I waited for my dream of total self-employment to come to fruition.

We all have dreams and desires. At times we spend countless hours dreaming of fulfilling them. We fall asleep with them on our minds, and we sometimes dream about them in the wee hours of the morning and then wake up with them at the forefront of our minds. We share our dreams with our best friends, and with our sisters, brothers, and mothers. Our significant others have heard about them repeatedly.

You have taken the time to write out your visions and to have an action plan and a timeline. Maybe you have even cut out a few pictures and placed them within your view so that you can focus on them throughout your day as a constant reminder to stay motivated. Some of you have done extensive research about what it would take to see your dreams and visions come true.

You have the support of your family, your friends, and your peers. You may have figured out all the changes you must make in your life to allow yourself the time needed to launch your dream vision. Family and friends may even have offered to take on some of your current responsibilities so that you can get started on your venture. For some reason, however, you find yourself sitting on the sidelines dreaming, wishing, and hoping for God to bless you and allow you to prosper. You know the old saying, "I'm waiting on God to move."

In order to turn your dream into your reality, you must get in the game. Become a participant in your dreams. Your time has come; do what you need to do so that you can reach your desired destination. If you plan to start a business, think of a suitable name and then apply for a business license. Have some cards printed or create them yourself. Maybe you want to obtain a degree. Once you have chosen your field, apply to a college, sign up for financial aid if you need it, and begin making the necessary adjustments in your schedule. If you dream of becoming active in your community, register to vote if you have not already done so, choose a cause that you are passionate about, and sign up as a volunteer.

Not every step that you take will be easy. There are always obstacles along the way, since life tends to throw a curveball occasionally. God's word, however, says that we must run with determination—meaning that, in spite of opposition, we are to continue with the action plan. Get into the game of your life's dreams and desires, determined that, no matter what—"Come hailstones or high water," as some used to say—you will keep on running.

Take the First Step

1. Sign up to participate in your game; take immediate action, and get started on one of your goals. What action can you take today to start working toward your goal?

_____

_____

_____

_____

_____

_____

_____

2. What resources do you need to begin working on your goals?

_____

_____

_____

_____

_____

_____

_____

3. Do not allow obstacles to discourage you; they cannot stop you. This is a time to call on God for his sustaining power. Write out a short prayer right now, asking God to give you knowledge, wisdom, and understanding as you pursue your dreams.

_____

_____

_____

_____

_____

_____

_____

_____

Focused Thought:

"You cannot win a race by sitting on the sidelines."

Carla's Coaching Challenge

Get into the game of your life. Stop sitting on the sidelines watching as others are prospering in the very things that you desire.

Journal Entry

Trying Times

I believed, therefore have I spoken: I was greatly afflicted.

—Psalm 116:10

There are times in our lives when our faith is tested. This seems especially true once you have set goals and start to accomplish them, moving forward, investing all your time and energy, giving it all that you have. It appears as if adversity is waiting around every corner for a prime opportunity to put a stop to all your hopes and dreams. It is during this time that we find ourselves beginning to have negative thoughts, wondering if we can gather any further strength to go on. We begin to speak against our dreams and ourselves, doubting our ability to continue on our God-ordained journey. Regardless of how large and heavy the struggle is, I challenge you to keep the faith.

I speak from experience, knowing firsthand the struggle of attempting to walk in the will of God against all odds. Having financial issues, relationship struggles, employment challenges, and family difficulties while trying to fulfill the call of God for your life is one thing, but enduring them all at the same time and having your health decline while trying to maintain a roof over your head is what you call "trying times."

Several years ago, while attempting to finish nursing school, I was diagnosed with an illness that left me without much strength or energy. I was unable to focus on my assignments and was unable keep up my grades. I was not able to graduate with the rest of my classmates, which left me discouraged. If that was not enough, I had to have two surgeries within a few months of one another.

I had to take medical leave because of the illness, which I had not prepared for financially because it had never dawned on me that I would ever really need short-term disability. There I found myself weak and in pain, with no money, and unable to care for myself financially or physically. On top of it all, I was in jeopardy of losing my house, my car, my job, and my ability to be independent.

All these struggles appeared in my life during a time when I felt I was walking in the will of God. I had felt that I was unstoppable. I was full of fire and zest, and then all of a sudden there were trials from every angle of my life. It was during this time that I made a decision simply to surrender to God's perfect plan and will for my life. I decided not to give up, but to trust that God was simply working everything out for his glory.

I have witnessed the struggle of many of my good friends who started out full of zeal, blessed and more than willing to go after what they felt was their God-given purpose, but who gave up too quickly at the first sign of struggles and setbacks. I have heard it said, "Struggles don't last always," but sometimes challenges come and are there for the long haul. Apostle Paul said, "Three times I pleaded with the Lord to take it away from me." God told Paul, however, "My grace is sufficient for you, for my power is made perfect in weakness" (2 Corinthians 12:8–9). The Bible tells us that faith *is* the substance. Faith is not contingent upon things going as expected or things going the way you thought they were supposed to go. The magic is in God having his way in bringing the result to pass.

Faith is, regardless of hurts, pains, rejections, sickness, debt, setbacks, failures, interference, or pure, calculated sabotage. Faith is the substance and the evidence. No matter what obstacle comes your way, you must strain forward. You may find yourself saying, "I am afflicted; I have no clue as to how I can continue." Nevertheless, faith is. You may find yourself saying, "Because of mounting debt, I will never be able to invest in my future." Nevertheless, faith is. You may find yourself saying, "I cannot do this because no one believes in me; I have no support system." Nevertheless, faith is. You may find yourself saying, "I cannot go any further because I am not smart enough, pretty enough, or perfect enough, nor do I have enough physical strength." Nevertheless, faith is. Faith travels much further than doubt. Faith is wiser, wealthier, and stronger than doubt or any struggle that opposing forces send your way.

Take the First Step

1. One of the hardest things to do while you believe in something is to wait. What can you do to increase your skills or add value to your life while you are waiting?

_____

_____

_____

_____

_____

_____

_____

2. Sometimes when you come to a point in your dream building, you stumble across obstacles that make you doubt God's plan for your life. Is there possibly something that God wants you to do differently or a change he desires in your life or behavior?

_____

_____

_____

_____

_____

_____

_____

_____

3. What can you do to be a blessing to someone else while you are waiting on your own blessing?

_____

_____

_____

_____

_____

_____

_____

_____

Focused Thought:

"Never give up on your dreams no matter what obstacles you have to face."

Carla's Coaching Challenge

Consider your wants and desires. Make sure that that they are in line up with the will of God for your life.

Journal Entry

Where Are You?

And the LORD God called unto Adam, and said unto him, Where art thou?

Genesis 3:9 (KJV)

I spent most of my life wearing a facade. For me, it was easy. I had a natural smile that said to the world that everything in my life was good. I hid behind the very thing that brought sunshine into the life of others. Everywhere I went I would get a compliment on my million-dollar smile. I often joke that I wish I could find a way to package and sell it. If the people who knew me back then only knew the truth behind the cover-up.

I was so not happy. I carried around so much pain and disappointment. I can remember people saying, "You are always happy and smiling." I know now that my smile is truly a gift from God because, no matter the condition of my life, it always remained intact. Not to say that there were not tears of sadness behind closed doors, but whenever I was in the presence of others my gift to shine light on them was more powerful than anything else in my life.

We all know, however, that you can only wear a facade for so long before the truth reveals itself. My revelation came about slowly as God's love began to shine so brightly in my life. The revelation of his love for me was so empowering that it felt as if God himself was calling out to me daily, "Carla, where are *you*?"

In 1996, I was attending classes to become a licensed practical nurse. I do not remember what led up to it, but I became depressed. I call it functional depression because I was functioning in life as always. I went to school and got mostly A's on my assignments. I went to work, and my home and family life were intact. So was my smile.

To the rest of the world, I was excelling, but when I was alone at home, I would close all the curtains and spend the day lying on my couch in the darkness. Sadness would engulf me. I did not have the desire to keep living, but my devotion to my God gave me the courage to hold on. I would get up the next day, attend classes and clinical, hang out with friends, and fix dinner or clean house as if my life was okay.

I can remember one day in particular when I was so close to complete darkness. The only thing left to do was to give in. I remember saying to God, "If you are real, then heal me." I stayed there at the foot of my bed for what could have been minutes or hours, I am not sure. But I do remember the sweet words that said to me, "You are healed."

I was finally able to shed the facade and let the real me come forth. The good news is that I was able to let go of the things I was covering up, but God allowed me to hold on to my smile. I truly believe that it is brighter now than ever before.

Do you know where you are in this life? Not only does God know where you are, but I believe that you too, know the truth about your current condition.

Some of you may be in a religious sanctuary, preaching the word of God or singing in the choir. You may be in a broken marriage or make-believe good marriage, where you and your mate sleep in separate beds each night. Some of you may be in an elite, Fortune 500 corporate environment or trying to make a name for yourself in your own entrepreneurial endeavor, earning the long-awaited six-figure income.

Others of you may be out raising money to feed the homeless, raising awareness for AIDS, or chairing one or two committees. Some may find themselves as welfare recipients, living a gay lifestyle, or spending their days drowning their sorrows in drugs or alcohol.

Maybe you are on your way to a stage play, driving your expensive car. You might be living a seemingly good life but somehow feel like something significant is missing. Or maybe you're retired, sitting on the fishing pier thanking God that you made it to the age you are now, considering the way that you lived your life.

God knows where you are physically, because he is right there beside you. He is with you all the way. The question, however, is where are *you*? What are you covering up? What condition are you really in? Why are you so far from the love that God is trying to pour into your life?

You may be living a lifestyle that allows you to walk around pretending that all is right in your world, living a life that allows you to cover up how you really feel. You may allow yourself to believe that you are okay with the pain that you live with each day.

The things that you try to cover up may be sin, shame, disappointments, fear, guilt, confusion, embarrassment, hatred, regrets, or even your desire to know whether God is real. Some people believe that if they belong to the right organizations, attend the right schools, go to church twice each week, and give to the poor, then everything is all right. At least they feel that they look all right to their peers, family, and friends.

God wants you to be aware of the condition you are in, because the longer you hide behind your cover-up, the longer you deny yourself a life of joy and abundance.

Acknowledge any sins, at least to yourself. Acknowledge any hurts, pains, disappointments, regrets, or lack of fulfillment.

If you look deeper, you may realize that you are living a life of low self-esteem, doubting yourself and regretting who you have become, lacking the self-confidence you need to make wiser choices. Once you unveil these hidden truths, you can face them head on and begin to open doors to living the life of your dreams.

Wherever you are and whatever you are doing, you will never be able to enjoy the full essence of your life until you acknowledge your true condition openly to God, with a willing heart, ready to allow God to turn your life around, toward the direction of true abundance.

Take the First Step

1. What unresolved issues have you tried to cover up or hide from yourself and the rest of the world that are secretly causing you pain or disappointment?

_____

_____

_____

_____

_____

_____

_____

2. Is there anyone that you need to forgive so that you can move forward in your life?

_____

_____

_____

_____

_____

_____

_____

3. Is there anyone that you have offended in any way that you need to make amends with so that you can move forward in your life in peace?

_____

_____

_____

_____

_____

_____

_____

_____

Focused Thought:

"Are you hiding behind elements of life, trying to hide the truth of what you are dealing with within your heart?"

Carla's Coaching Challenge

Take time to deal with the truth and with any unresolved issues in your life. It is not necessary to reveal everything to other people, but it will benefit you to be honest with yourself. Once you are honest with yourself, release these truths to God in confession and prayer, and trust him to mend the broken areas of your heart.

Journal Entry

It's All about You

These are the things you are to do: Speak the truth to each other ...

—Zechariah 8:16

Whenever you voice a concern or give an opinion to someone, always say exactly what you feel. Tell the truth when you speak, whatever it is that you believe in you heart. This may require that you take a stand, refusing to step outside your boundaries in order to satisfy the needs of others. How you feel matters. What you have decided that you want for your life matters. Once you set out to fulfill your goals and live the life of your dreams, do not let anyone else determine the road that you shall travel.

This is a very important matter, because if you stop speaking your truth, you begin to cut yourself into tiny little pieces, day after day. It could get to the point that you no longer trust or believe in yourself. You will begin to doubt every decision that you make—that is, if you even trust yourself to make decisions anymore.

I have found from personal experience that whenever I give up my right to speak my own truths, what I am really doing is giving control of my life to others. Once you give away control, your self-esteem becomes depleted, which can lead to self-destructive behaviors. You will suddenly find yourself blaming others for your disappointments. You might find yourself becoming bitter, angry, and resentful. These feelings, if not dealt with, can lead to anxiety, depression, and loneliness, because you no longer trust yourself or the people around you.

Remember that you are somebody important; your opinions matters. Your voice has power, and using it to speak your truth will keep your mind and spirit at peace. Sometimes those closest to us and those who are trying to give us a helping hand may mean well by offering advice or offering a great opportunity, but stick to your gut feeling if what they are offering does not line up with your purpose, goals, and desires—the way you have decided to live your life. Most important, do not silence your voice in hopes of obtaining love or acceptance from anyone. If you must become someone you are not or do things that are not in alignment with your values and beliefs, consider what you are giving up before you allow yourself to step outside your own boundaries.

Maintain your dignity; determine your own self-worth; take a stand for your right to be who God created you to be. Allow the person you are to be in harmony with whatever you do, how you act, and what you say. Always surrender to the spirit of God within you to find your truths. Speak these truths at all times. Never step outside your boundaries, and never give up control to anyone. It's all about you and the life that God has created you to live.

Take the First Step

1. Can you think of a time when you did not speak up and tell someone how you really felt about a certain situation?

   _____

   _____

   _____

   _____

   _____

   _____

   _____

   _____

2. Is there something that you are doing right now outside your value system because you refused to speak up for yourself?

   _____

   _____

   _____

   _____

   _____

   _____

   _____

   _____

3. Make an affirmation right now that you will speak your truth concerning your life and what you desire.

   _____

   _____

   _____

   _____

   _____

_____

_____

_____

_____

Focused Thought:

"What you have to say matters."

Carla's Coaching Challenge

The next time you find yourself keeping quiet when you have something important to say, speak up.

Journal Entry

A New Life Attitude

We shall go up and take possession of the land, for we can certainly do it.

Numbers 13:30

Your attitude is the determining factor as to whether or not you will live the life of your dreams. Do you possess a can-do attitude concerning your dreams and life's purpose? Have you made up your mind to overcome the giants in your life, the major obstacles standing in the way of your living out the promises of God for your life?

As children of God, we have his spirit at work within us, renewing our faith day by day. Christ's main objective on earth was to give us life—a life full of joy and abundance. What is stopping you from living that abundant life? Could it be a negative attitude toward life?

Your attitude determines how far you will travel in life, it determines your level of growth, and it determines whether you will speak positively or negatively about your future. What is holding you back from living the abundant life you deserve and desire? Could it be a limited attitude, limited thoughts, or old ways of doing things? Perhaps old behaviors and past mistakes are holding you back.

You will never reach your true potential, achieve your dreams, or live out your visions thinking the way you did yesterday. Isaiah 43:18 states, "Forget the former things; do not dwell on the past." What are some old things that are holding you back? Could it be fear, or a feeling of not being good enough or smart enough? Maybe it is because you feel your resources and money supply are limited.

Do you allow your gender or race to stop you from moving forward, or the fact that you feel that you are too old, too young or maybe have too many kids? Remember that God is doing something new. Do not let the fear of being intimidated, or having an introverted nature, stop you from claiming and taking hold of the promises of God.

God promised you a land flowing with provisions for your life. If you allow what appears to be too big for you to conquer to put fear in you and hold you back, and persuade you to give up on your hopes and dreams, you will become stagnant. You must realize that what appear to be giants in your life, what appears to be overwhelming, is really insignificant compared to what God has placed inside you: the ability to move mountains.

You have the ability to remove major obstacles just by changing the way you view the object in your way. Up close, it appears a massive mountain, but step away a few feet, and you will realize it is nothing more than a nugget. You can step right over it, pick it up and toss it to the side, or crush it as you continue walking in the direction of your dreams.

You must see things from a new standpoint. You must allow new thoughts of victory to accompany you on your journey to your promised land. Get rid of the old way of thinking, the limiting thoughts, and the old attitude. Declare today that you will have a positive new life attitude.

Take the First Step

1. Write in the space below about the lifestyle you feel you deserve and desire.

_____

_____

_____

_____

_____

_____

_____

2. Write at least three affirming promises of God concerning the abundant life you deserve and desire. (Search the scriptures.)

_____

_____

_____

_____

_____

_____

_____

3. What wrong attitude do you need to let go of in order to walk into the new areas of your life?

_____

_____

_____

_____

_____

_____

_____

Focused Thought:

"You must believe in your God-given ability to succeed in order to create the life that you desire."

Carla's Coaching Challenge

Start expecting a positive outcome concerning every goal or affirmation that you set for yourself.

Journal Entry

Maintain Your Strength

But the people that do know their God shall be strong,
and do exploits.

—Daniel 11:32 (KJV)

To live a life of integrity is to live in complete truthfulness and
sincerity- an authentic life. It is living in a state of totality and
soundness. Integrity is present in your life when your actions
are consistent with your internal beliefs. In order to live the
life of your dreams, it is essential that you live a lifestyle of
integrity.

Living a life of integrity is a choice, one that you must
make on a day-to-day, minute-to-minute basis. As you begin
the life of your dreams, you will find yourself having to make
some difficult decisions. People and situations will sometimes
appear flattering, causing you to vacillate between right and
wrong. Sometimes offers come your way that seem too good to
be true. People who are in financial debt may find themselves
choosing to walk a path that is not in line with their personal
mission or vision. All these are ways that you may compromise
your integrity.

To know God is to be intimate with him. Spend quality
time getting to know his ways. Pray to him daily, especially

when you find yourself at a crossroads, in need of spiritual wisdom. Friends and experts are great resources; actually, they are necessary during your time of growth and development. However, there will be times in your life when no one else can decide "the way" for you except you. Your relationship with God will prove to be the source of your strength, the key to your wholeness and a constant reminder of your purpose for being.

Not only will you be successful yourself; you will also be in a position to empower, inspire, and instruct in the way of wisdom others whom God has placed in your path. Those who stand firm and maintain their strength and their integrity will do great exploits for God. So, maintain your strength and your power by making an unyielding decision to live a lifestyle of integrity, one that your friends, family and greatest fans can admire and emulate.

Take the First Step

1. In the past, in what ways have you compromised your integrity?

_____

_____

_____

_____

_____

_____

_____

2. Make a list of people that you admire—people who exhibit integrity.

_____

_____

_____

_____

_____

_____

_____

_____

3.   What would your friends and family say about the
     way you conduct yourself?

_____

_____

_____

_____

_____

_____

_____

_____

Focused Thought:

"As you grow in your relationship with God, you will be
encouraged to live a life of integrity."

Carla's Coaching Challenge

Choose to live each day with integrity. Think about everything
that you do and say, then ask yourself, *Am I being true to who
I really am?*

Journal Entry

Consider Your Ways

Blessed is the man who does not walk in the counsel
of the wicked or stand in the way of sinners or sit in
the seat of mockers. But his delight is in the law of the
Lord, and on his law he meditates day and night. He
is like a tree planted by streams of water, which yields
fruit in season and whose leaf does not wither.

—Psalm 1:1–3

Your spirit is your true life. Sin brings death to your spirit.
There is no other way to say it; sin will destroy you. What
sin does is eat away at your self-esteem; it will bring about
unnecessary anxieties in your life. It will eat away at your
dreams and hopes. Sin will interrupt your rest; it tears down the
spirit of those who God entrusted in your care—your family,
spouse, children, and friends. Consider your ways: are they
causing you to be stagnant in life? I am not trying to inflict
personal judgment on anyone; what I am suggesting is that you
think about everything you do and every decision you make.
How will they affect those around you?

There is a promise of happiness, good fortune, and
overall prosperity to those who do not follow wickedness or
wrongdoing. Most of us desire to have our dreams manifested;

we desire fame and fortune, good health, and long life. Most of us also long to assist others in fulfilling their purpose in life. What it all really boils down to is happiness. The reason most people seek these things is a lifelong search for true happiness. True happiness comes by following God's law and living life with God-like characteristics.

If you desire happiness in your life, choose not to sin, choose not to follow the advice of those who take sin lightly, as if there is no separation between good and bad or right and wrong. Those who choose to set themselves apart from an immoral lifestyle will be as a tree planted by the river; they will have an unfailing supply of refreshment, nourishment, and happiness.

A well-watered tree is strong, healthy, vibrant, and full of delicious fruit and beautiful green leaves. That is the ultimate description of a happy person. There is abundance of life in the choice you make to live a sin-free life. Your choices have power to cause you to prosper. Appropriate actions will cause your hopes and dreams to manifest far beyond what you can imagine or hope.

Our spiritual being will always experience a variety of feelings. One day we will find ourselves feeling happy, the next day, sad. At times, we feel on top of the mountain; the next moment we are at the lowest point of the valley. People who take the time to consider their ways and choose a lifestyle that allows them to hold their heads up high—a lifestyle of integrity, a lifestyle that brings joy and good tidings to themselves, their family, and their community, a God-centered life—will be stable, unshakable, and able to endure and prosper in all ways.

Take the first Step

1. When you are in need of advice, where do you go to seek guidance?

   _____

   _____

   _____

   _____

   _____

   _____

   _____

   _____

2. Do you have any questionable behaviors that may stand in the way of the many blessings that God wants to send your way?

   _____

   _____

   _____

   _____

   _____

   _____

   _____

3. Are there any people in your life at this time that you need to reconsider as friends, confidants, and advisors?

   _____

   _____

   _____

   _____

   _____

_____

_____

_____

_____

Focused Thought:

"Meditating on the principles of God will add value to your life."

Carla's Coaching Challenge

The next time you are looking for a solution to a problem in your life, try reading Bible verses that speak about what you are dealing with at that time.

Journal Entry

Your Gifts Will Open Doors

A gift opens the way for the giver and ushers him into
the presence of the great.

—Proverbs 18:16

Having a dream that sets your heart on fire and a desire to share
that dream with the world, but not knowing how to position
yourself among those who are already experts in your field can
be frustrating. You may find yourself spending countless hours,
days, and months trying to figure out how to get your name out,
how to make yourself known, attending seminars to learn how
to expose your gifts and talents to the right people.

The word of God states that your gift will open doors for
you and position you in the presence of great men. Even if no
one knows you, find out what is going on in the places you are
trying to go. Talk to everyone you meet—a receptionist, the
person at the ticket booth at a conference you are attending.
Strike up a conversation while you are riding the bus or train.
Tell all your family and friends what it is you're doing. Everyone
knows someone else; do not take anyone for granted. I have
found that everyone has something to offer, some good advice
and some bad. You never know whether the person with whom

you are speaking holds the key to the door you have been trying to open, or has access to the person who does.

In the beginning, you may have to offer your services as gift. Give away your time, your services, become a volunteer with someone else who is doing what you desire to do. Remember that the people who are experts and are well known are busy people. These are great men and women whose time is limited. People who are looking to promote their own cause probably approach them daily. That is why it is important to be kind to everyone; you never know whether the person sitting beside you on the bus is the best friend, confidant, or receptionist of the great people you are trying to meet.

Remember to share your gifts with the world; let your gift be your voice. It is not how many degrees you have; they do not promise you a key to the palace among the great. Everyone, however, is enticed by a gift. All people like to receive something of value. If you are feeling inadequate or have previously tried to sell yourself, based on your accomplishments, but failed to make any headway, trust in the unique gifts and talents that God has given you. Allow your gift and your talents to announce you to the world; do not worry about monetary rewards. The gift will open doors for you. Your gifts and talents will position you among those of power and influence.

Take the First Step

1. When trying to market yourself or your product or services, what of value can you offer to others?

_____

_____

_____

_____

_____

_____

_____

2. Are you aware of your natural gifts and talents? List them below.

_____

_____

_____

_____

_____

_____

_____

_____

3. In what ways can you be of assistance to others as you are waiting for doors of opportunity to open for you?

_____

_____

_____

_____

_____

_____

_____

Focused Thought:

"You never know where your gift will lead you."

Carla's Coaching Challenge

Figure out exactly what you have to offer and share that with the world.

Journal Entry

Express Yourself

It is written: "I believed; therefore I have spoken."
With that same spirit of faith we also should believe
and therefore speak.

—Corinthians 4:13

Our voice has more power than the credit it is given. Our dreams begin in our heart. From there we pen them on paper so that they appear more real to us. It is not until we speak them, however, that they begin to take form. God said, and whatever he said appeared. Not only did it appear; but it was good.

Your voice has a purpose. Your purpose is to speak the truths that God has revealed to you. Others may not always agree with what you have to say, but you still have the right to say what you feel.

When you speak your dreams, you give life to them. You have taken the time to think about your dreams and desires; you have spent hours, days, and months meditating on your new life. You have sought God and written out your plans. Maybe you have simply written in your journal your deepest desires; maybe you have fully written out your goals and objectives or have written a full business plan. The next thing to do is begin to speak them. Talk about them to everyone of interest.

God's word tells you to be bold and courageous. Even when you are low on faith and obstacles are coming from every direction, keep talking. If you truly believe in the authentic vision given to you by God, you must use the power of the spoken word to express yourself. Have faith in what God has revealed to you, trust that what he has shown you will indeed happen for you. If you believe, then speak. Trust the sound of your own voice. Your voice counts; it matters. It has the ability to give life to your dreams.

Remember, you are unique; your dreams are unique to you. The path you are to travel is unique. So is the sound of your spoken words, your own thoughts, and your voice. Express yourself; overcome the fear of your own voice.

Take the First Step

1. What promises or visions do you feel that God has spoken into your life?

_____

_____

_____

_____

_____

_____

_____

2. Rewrite these promises or vision below in the form of an affirmation.

_____

_____

_____

_____

_____

_____

_____

_____

3. With whom can you share your dreams and
    visions?

_____

_____

_____

_____

_____

_____

_____

_____

_____

Focused Thought:

"No matter what challenges come your way, continue to speak
life to your dreams."

Carla's Coaching Challenge

Start each day by speaking your dreams out loud.

Journal Entry

Stay on the Path

Teach me thy way, O LORD: lead me in a straight
path.

—Psalms 27:11

In order to live the authentic and abundant life you deserve
and desire, you must have a mind-set to stand firm in the face
of opposition. You must maintain a positive attitude and be
determined to overcome whatever negative forces lie in your
path.

Your dreams and your life's mission are given to you by
God. Along with the dreams, he has given you all the power
you need to manifest these dreams. God is with you all the
way. Knowing that he is there and will never leave you alone
or helpless should give you the courage to endure.

Anyone determined to win in life will be faced with
opposition along the way. There is no way around it. The only
thing you can do is be strong and courageous. Most important,
do not give up.

Remember all that you have learned in the past. Do whatever
it takes to fight off the opposing forces. Fight back by using
your God-given talents and gifts—whatever has worked for you
in the past. If you are dealing with illness and physical pain, see

your doctor immediately and follow his or her advice, whether that means medication, meditation, exercises, or eating right; just do it.

If you have a setback in your life due to loss of a job, loss of a loved one, the end of a relationship, or financial hardship, take time to breathe. Reevaluate where you are in your life, then make plans to move on to the next stage of your life, whether this means taking time out to heal or to regroup or figure out where you could have went wrong or made mistakes.

In order to live a life of courage and boldness in the face of opposition, you must maintain a positive attitude at all times. There is no room for negativism. Stay focused on the dream, on your purpose. There are people who are waiting for you to succeed in order that they may have a positive mentor to help them overcome obstacles and fulfill their own life's purpose.

Most important, remember that you are not alone on this journey. God promises never to leave you or forsake you. He has already prepared the way for you. Nothing can stop what God has put into motion. Nothing can overthrow God's plan for your life. When you are at your weakest, remember that he is your strength.

Sometimes your own mind will speak against your plans, but if you store God's words in your heart, they will be there to see you through. Prayer is the key to silencing opposing forces of the mind, along with courage and boldness to continue on the path. There may be times when you become sidetracked and lose your way, but know that God is the lamp that lights the way.

Take the First Step

1. What opposition are you facing in your life right now?

_____

_____

_____

_____

_____

_____

_____

2. List three things that you can do now to assist you in getting past this opposition.

_____

_____

_____

_____

_____

_____

_____

3. Take a moment to pray. What do you want God to do for you concerning this situation?

_____

_____

_____

_____

_____

_____

_____

Focused Thought:

"God is the key; prayer is the method to keeping your focus in trying times."

Carla's Coaching Challenge

If ever your life is out of balance, pray. Seek God for direction.

Journal Entry

Say Good-bye

Jesus replied, "No one who puts his hand on the plow and looks back is fit for service in the kingdom of God."

—Luke 9:62

Yes, you are a person of action. The future is yours to conquer. No obstacle in front of you can stop you. You hold the tools in your hands needed to create and live the life of your dreams. You possess creative abilities; armed with multiple talents and skills. Your faith will take you as far as your mind can imagine. You are beautiful, full of grace, intelligent, and loved beyond measure. Nothing can take away your power as long as you keep your vision on the future, in the direction that God is leading.

Let the past have its place, behind you. Do not waste your energy focusing on yesterday. Looking back can draw you out of position. You will be apt to go back to things that you have already said good-bye to.

You may have let go of a worldly existence, or maybe you have let go of past rejections, hurts, and disappointments. Maybe you have let go of a job or something else in your life that no longer holds your interest. The past could be family or friends who have constantly hurt you or did not value you as a person. Sometimes leaving the past behind is simply about following your dreams and going after your heart's desires. Whatever you left in the past, leave it there, and do not look back.

Those who have not decided to break from the past are not ready to sow into the territory of future dreams. You must break loose from the past before you can be successful in obtaining the things you desire for your future. Holding on to the past could be stopping you from living your dreams and fulfilling your purpose. It may require forgiving yourself or someone else. It may simply require making a decision not to look back. But by all means necessary, do what needs to be done, then press forward to the things that you desire in your future.

Do not give away your power to the past. You can sow your seeds of desire into the empty places that need filling, that void that remained when you decided to leave the past behind. Stay focused on God and his plan for your life, and you will see the results of your actions. Keep your focus on your future goals and priorities. You will end up in the place that you focus on. Look toward the future, and maintain a one-way path.

Take the First Step

1. What or who in your life do you feel that you must release and leave in your past in order to move forward into your future?

_____

_____

_____

_____

_____

_____

_____

2. Is there anything that you have let go of previously that you are tempted to go back to that may interfere with your dreams and desire?

_____

_____

_____

_____

_____

_____

_____

_____

3. What situation or person do you need to forgive so that you can be free to fulfill your dreams?

_____

_____

_____

_____

_____

_____

_____

_____

Focused Thought:

"The answers to your dreams are in front of you."

Carla's Coaching Challenge

Let go of past mistakes and disappointment. Forgive yourself and others for past transgressions. Learn from the past, but live your life in the future.

Journal Entry

It's Not Really about You!

A man's life does not consist in the abundance of his possessions.

—Luke 12:15

Sometimes as we go about our lives trying to fulfill our purpose we may find ourselves frustrated. During these times, our prayer can become somewhat selfish. We begin to desire possessions, fame, and fortune. We may find ourselves disappointed, day after day, when we realize that the things that we desire in life appear much easier for others to obtain but remain out of our reach. We grow tired of waiting for the manifestations of our dreams, forgetting that we are just an instrument, used by God for a greater purpose.

This is a revelation for me even as I write this chapter. I feel overwhelmed because my dreams are big, but feel so far out of my grasp. I have planned; I have done as much as I know how to do at this time. I have even designed the front and back cover of this book as an inspiration to myself. I have a vision board, a Web site, a logo, and stationery. I am an introvert who has learned to speak up and speak out. A few hours ago, however, I was discouraged—mad, even—because I am still in debt and nobody knows who I am or what I feel I have to offer. I am not sure whether I can even write a book. I am not even sure what to do with it after it is completed.

After rereading this scripture, God's word began to remind me that it is not all about me. It is not about what I want, what I can or cannot do, or who I think I am. Time or things do not belong to me. God is the source of all things. Do not forget to seek God's kingdom first. Dwell in his presence, marvel at his goodness, and all the other things that you desire will come.

His word also reminds me that everything that I have need of, I already have. We must remember that God gives us the desires of our heart, meaning that all the good that we desire to do comes from him. Therefore, if God is the giver of the gift, we must trust his way and his timing in allowing all that we desire to manifest. Most important, we must remember why. Why did God give you your vision? Your vision is part of God's greater plan for humanity. Your purpose is to be a blessing to those that God put in your path. It's not really all about you.

Take the First Step

1. What are you trying to accomplish right now that sometimes leaves you feeling frustrated?

_____

_____

_____

_____

_____

_____

_____

_____

2. What are your grateful for in your life at this very
    moment?

_____

_____

_____

_____

_____

_____

_____

_____

3. Think of one person whom you can bless right now
    using your natural talents and gifts.

_____

_____

_____

_____

_____

_____

_____

_____

Focused Thought:

"It is not all about what's in it for you, but how what you possess
can be of use, as a resource, to bless others."

Carla's Coaching Challenge

The next time you find yourself frustrated because things are
not happening for you as quickly as you would like, take a
moment to remember that everything happens according to
God's timing and for the highest good of all.

Journal Entry

Fear is Not an Option

Don't be afraid; just believe.

—Mark 5:36

Sometimes your own thoughts can be an obstacle. Having thoughts of fear, rejection, or failure can stop you from believing in your dreams. Having your thoughts clouded with fear of success, living life alone, or thinking you are not good enough could stop you from even trying to succeed. One thing you can do is follow the example of the wisest man who ever lived—Jesus.

In the Book of Mark, he overhears some people telling a man that his daughter is dead and that there is no need to bother the Master. They are speaking of the teacher, Jesus. Jesus ignores the words of those speaking, however, and says to the man, "Be not afraid, just keep believing." Jesus ignores all the negative reports he hears; he ignores the report of others.

You, too, must ignore all negative reports coming not only from the people around you, but also from your own mind. There will be times when it feels hopeless, times where it may seem useless to continue with your dreams, your priorities, and your objectives. It is at this point that you must say to yourself that fear is not an option.

When hopelessness is in your thoughts, God will show up as promised and show you a way to succeed at whatever it is you are trying to accomplish at that time. It is only possible, however, if you believe. If your answer is yes, it is possible, then the word of God says, "According to your faith, will it be done to you" (Mathew 9:29). You must exercise your faith when it appears that there is no hope.

There may even come a time when it appears that you have lost everything. Maybe you have lost a marriage, your job, or your finances have become depleted. The people who started out believing in you may be long gone. Do not think that the words of encouragement that God is speaking to you are all in vain.

It is at this time that you must hear from deep within your own spirit the words of life spoken to you. No matter how bleak things look, there will always—and I repeat, always—be a spark of light, a ray of sunshine, a glimmer of hope revealed to you. All you have to do is believe and open your heart to receive.

If you only believe, keep the faith; then God can and will do the impossible. Search your heart for possibilities concerning your situation. Surround yourself with other believers, people who believe in you and have strong faith, who also believe in what is possible.

Take the First Step

1. Are you praying for God to do something special in your life? If so, what is it?

_____

_____

_____

_____

_____

_____

_____

_____

2. Write out a positive affirmation about your special
   prayer?

_____

_____

_____

_____

_____

_____

_____

3. What negative reports that others have spoken to
   you do you need to let go of?

_____

_____

_____

_____

_____

_____

_____

Focused Thought:

"Do not fear outward circumstances that you see or hear."

Carla's Coaching Challenge

When you begin to have doubts and fears concerning your
hopes and dreams, begin to exercise your faith by speaking
positively about your situation.

Journal Entry

Take the First Step

The king said to me, "What is it you want?" Then I
prayed to the God of heaven.

—Nehemiah 2:4

The first step to living the life of your dreams is to know
what you want. You cannot get to where you are going without
knowing what it is you are seeking. If someone asked you
today, "What is it that you want?" would you be able to give
an answer without much thought? If not, then everything else
needs to be put on hold until you figure it out. Otherwise you
will find yourself at another dead-end in your life, completely
unfulfilled.

Figuring out what you want is not as hard as you may think.
Pay attention to what bothers you, what upsets you, or what
gets you excited.

Is your heart particularly fond of children, the elderly,
women, men, or a particular race? Does injustice make you
fume? Maybe you have more than compassion for the sick and
desire to fill their hearts with hope. Perhaps you have a love of
fashion and have been dressing dolls all your life. Do you have
a creative flair, or do you find yourself growing flowers in your
garden? Do you take pride in arranging them in beautiful vases

once they are in full bloom? Think about that special project or activity that you look forward to doing whenever you have free time. If you are still perplexed, the Bible reminds us that "God gives us the desires of our heart" (Psalm 37:4).

Spend time in prayer and meditation, seeking God for your desires and for your purpose. Ask him why he allowed you to be born, what purpose he has for you. God will begin to stir up the gifts, the desires within you. Be open to receiving what comes into your focus; pay attention to your intuition. Get out and try new things; be around a variety of people. Pay attention to how others respond to you. What is it that your family and friends constantly compliment you on? Just remember that your vision is greater than you are. Not only will it bring you joy and pleasure; it will also be a blessing to others.

Someone is in need of your gifts, your vision. Someone else's vision depends on you fulfilling yours. Your true vision is pleasing in the sight of God. Take the time to answer the question, what is it that you want? Until you identify it and answer it directly and with clarity, you will remain stagnant and unfulfilled.

Take the First Step

1. What clues show up in your life that gives you an idea about what you want for your life?

_____

_____

_____

_____

_____

_____

_____

2. If someone asked you right now what you wanted out of your life, what would you say?

_____

_____

_____

_____

_____

_____

_____

3. What compliments do you usually get from your family, friends, and co-workers?

_____

_____

_____

_____

_____

_____

_____

Focused Thought:

"If someone wanted to grant you the one desire of your heart, but only if you could tell him or her that desire in three seconds, would you be able to answer?"

Carla's Coaching Challenge

Take time to figure out what you want for your life. You never know when someone will be in the position to help you achieve it.

Journal Entry

Joy, Joy, Joy

Hope deferred makes the heart sick, but a longing fulfilled is a tree of life.

—Proverbs 13:12

One of the most frustrating things in life is to anticipate something and not know what it is you really desire. Has that ever happened to you? Have you ever found yourself restless, wishing for more, wanting more? Have you ever had a feeling that you were born to do something great? I believe it is a sign that God is tugging at your heart, requesting you to seek him for revelation of the craving deep down in your soul.

Psalm 37:4 states, "Delight yourself in the Lord and he will give you the desires of your heart." To delight in anything is to be content with something, to be thrilled by it, and to exult. If you delight yourself in God, he will reveal to you those secret longings of your heart. If you make him the delight of your heart, he in return will reveal to you your life's purpose.

Once you receive the revelation of your desires, this discovery becomes a tree of life. It satisfies the longing and becomes a source of happiness for you. The known desire becomes a source of everlasting joy. You will feel as if you have finally gotten the assignment that you have waited for your whole life. Along with this assignment come provisions for your life and the life of those in your care.

A tree of life is always fruitful. Once you receive the revelation of your desires, expect great things to happen in your life. Life as usual will cease to be. You will now live a life of excitement and expectation, looking forward to the beginning of each new day.

Sometimes the desire is delayed, which can cause you to despair and think about giving up on discovering your passions and fulfilling your life's purpose. Do not give up, do not give in, remember that God is in control of the appointed time for the manifestation of your desires.

Pray, and trust God to fulfill his promise. Also, realize that waiting builds character, maturity, and patience. Waiting teaches you to persevere and allows you to appreciate the fulfillment once you have received it. Romans 5:5 states, "And hope does not disappoint us." Know also that the outside manifestation of your desires, your dreams, your vision, your life's purpose will become a tree of life for others. You will be in a position to help those whom God has placed in your life. Your desires will bring about tremendous love, support, provision, and happiness for others in the world.

Take the First Step

1. What does it mean to delight in the Lord?

_____

_____

_____

_____

_____

_____

_____

_____

2. In what ways can you delight (enjoy, find pleasure, get to know intimately) yourself in God?

_____

_____

_____

_____

_____

_____

_____

3. What is your current relationship with God? Do you spend time in prayer, acknowledging his presence and existence?

_____

_____

_____

_____

_____

_____

_____

Focused Thought:

"The source of your joy lies in your relationship with God."

Carla's Coaching Challenge

Develop an intimate relationship with God. The greatest knowledge, wisdom, and understanding of love and life come from him.

Journal Entry

The Truth of the Matter

Do everything in love.

—1 Corinthians 16:14

Everyone has a unique purpose in life, as well as different talents and gifts. Your ultimate purpose in life is to provide a service to others. I am not speaking merely of doing a good deed. I am talking about genuine love, inspired by the very love of God, who first loved us. Because of God's love for us, we now have the opportunity to live an abundant life. We in return should show love to our fellow man—our brother, our sister, our neighbor. There is no greater way to acknowledge gratitude for such a great life than to live your life in devotion to God and those that you encounter throughout your lifetime.

Although love is the ultimate gift, the most enormous gift that any man can give to another, it costs us so little. Actually, sharing love costs us nothing. All that is required is that we carry a bagful of this precious gift with us each day and distribute it into the hearts of everyone we encounter. If you stumble upon someone who has fallen, take a minute to help him or her up with an encouraging word. If you happen to run into someone who is lost, take the time to show him or her the way. Maybe you will visit someone and find that person sitting in the dark.

If you are able, assist him or her by restoring the lights in their home, literally and figuratively. Whatever your job is in this world, whatever you do on a daily basis to provide for yourself and your family, be sure to do it with love.

The purpose of sharing love is to give life and hope to others. Jesus came and died that we may have and enjoy life. Your purpose in life is also to give life to others. Success is not simply for selfish reasons; success comes to expand your opportunities to help others grow and have abundance in life. Give, and it shall return to you. The more love you give to others, the more love God will allow to flow into your life. Just be sure to give out of love for God and his children.

A deed performed with kindness and generosity lives forever. It flows through the heart of the receiver like magic; it has power to heal, increase faith, and restore joy and hope. Service performed in love opens the heart of the receiver to accept you, which will allow you to become a mentor and share all that you know with that person.

Take the First Step

1. Make a decision to have an attitude of love as you perform whatever duties are required of you. Write an affirmation of your decision to have an attitude of love toward everyone that you encounter throughout your day.

_____

_____

_____

_____

_____

_____

_____

2. Look for opportunities to offer a word of encouragement or assistance to everyone you encounter. Who do you know that is in need of your encouragement or assistance?

_____

_____

_____

_____

_____

_____

_____

3. Take every opportunity to share the greatest gift of all, the gift of love. In what way can you share the gift of love with someone else today?

_____

_____

_____

_____

_____

_____

_____

Focused Thought:

"There is no greater gift than love."

Carla's Coaching Challenge

Make it your No. 1 purpose in life to give the gift of love wherever you go.

Journal Entry

Delight in His Will

> "My food," said Jesus, "is to do the will of him who sent me and to finish his work."
>
> John 4:34

Have you ever heard the saying, "You get what you pay for"? Some people waste a whole lifetime trying to obtain riches. They travel around the world or spend large sums of money on the next get-rich-quick seminar. Others spend half of their lives attending college after college, trying to add to their credentials in order that they may request a higher salary from their employer. If you go after these things with all that is in you, chances are that you will obtain them. You can only experience true satisfaction, however, as you work to fulfill the will of God for your life.

There is nothing wrong with desiring riches or obtaining further education; they come in handy in this life. We should first seek the will of God for our lives, however, and everything that we desire for our lives will come in time. Like natural food for the body, money and education bring satisfaction for a short period. They may afford you great luxuries and increase your status among men. Once you obtain these things and use them for your desired purposes, however, you will again feel the hunger pain of being unfulfilled.

You will find yourself trying to acquire the next level of wealth, status, or fame—trying repeatedly to obtain the same pleasure, only to realize that it is never enough. These gains alone will never satisfy the longing of the heart.

For those of us in search of true happiness and long-lasting satisfaction, we should only look to the example of the wisest man who ever lived, Christ. His food, his nourishment, came from following God's will for his life.

Food is a substance that enables you to live and grow. We all have need of natural food so that our physical bodies do not perish, just as we need resources to purchase our homes and clothe our families. Today's society requires that we have cars and planes to travel from place to place. In order to obtain these things, we must have money. The higher our education, the more money we usually earn.

Having a business that is a success is also a great resource for acquiring what we need. It is not wrong to desire abundance, but realize that these things do not take the place of God's ultimate will for your life.

As disciples of Christ, we have a mandate to win lost souls. What I am saying, and what God's word confirms, is that we are not only to concern ourselves with earning a wage in life, but also with gathering souls for eternal life, which is our true purpose.

God desires to use you in your everyday life—your occupation, your relationships, and your hobbies. He will not only bring great blessings into your life; he also desires to use you in ways that are bigger than you could ever imagine.

Take the First Step

1. What do you feel is God's ultimate purpose for your life?

_____

_____

_____

_____

_____

_____

_____

2. Are there times in your life when you feel totally unfulfilled and believe there is something more that you should be doing?

_____

_____

_____

_____

_____

_____

_____

3. In what areas of your life do you need to allow God to direct your decisions?

_____

_____

_____

_____

_____

_____

_____

Focused Thought:

"By surrendering your life to God's will, you will open the way for God to lead, direct, and bless you and those he has placed in your care."

Carla's Coaching Challenge

Say a prayer of surrender to the will of God. Know that his love for you is unconditional. When you are ready to live a life of purpose and passion, he will lead you to a place of tranquility and multitudes of blessings.

Journal Entry

Embrace Your Uniqueness

I praise you because I am fearfully and wonderfully
made; your works are wonderful.

—Psalm 139:14

Sometimes we find it hard to look at ourselves in the mirror
and smile back at what we see, not because we are disfigured
or scarred or even unpleasant to the eye. We sometimes dislike
the way we look simply because we look nothing like the people
on TV or in the magazines or the well-put-together, size-six
top executive or GQ model. We put ourselves through undue
misery by comparing ourselves to the image that the world has
declared as beauty and fame.

You, as God's jewels, must refrain from letting vanity
or wealth determine your true essence. Brilliantly and
magnificently, God created you, and marvelous is the creation
of God. The Creator constructed you before birth, while you
were but a speck in your mother's womb. God personally formed
and fashioned you into someone beautiful and amazing. Each
one of you was born into this world with your own individual
characteristics and unique qualities.

You are a work of art, created with unique specifications, formed by the master's hand. Duplicating art decreases its value, but an original piece of artwork is priceless.

A special mother in my home church used to say, "If God had made you to be like someone else, then who would be you?" How true indeed. You are an original, and the world would be missing a masterpiece if you became like someone else. Embrace your uniqueness.

God knew you when you were unformed, in your imperfect state, yet his thoughts toward you were of love and admiration. Those who care about you—your family, children, spouse, and friends—love and appreciate your beauty and worth. So why spend your time wishing to be like someone else or wishing to remove the very details that make you a unique, priceless masterpiece.

Take the First Step

1. Make a list of all of your special achievements.

_____

_____

_____

_____

_____

_____

_____

_____

2. What special qualities do you have that make you different from everyone else? What is it that your family and your close friends love about you?

_____

_____

_____

_____

_____
_____
_____
_____

3. In what way can you, as an individual, give back
    to the world or to those who are less fortunate than
    you are?

_____
_____
_____
_____
_____
_____
_____
_____

Focused Thought:

"God found you to be such a beautiful, unique jewel that he
decided to birth you into the world as a gift to others."

Carla's Coaching Challenge

Take all your faults, failures, and flaws and combine them with
your gifts, talents, and abilities. What you will end up with is a
recipe for success and fulfillment for your life and a unique gift
to offer to the rest of the world. Embrace that gift.

Journal Entry

_____

_____

_____

_____

_____

_____

_____

_____

_____

_____

_____

_____

_____

_____

_____

_____

_____

_____

_____

_____

_____

_____

_____

_____

_____

_____

_____

Doing Things God's Way

Blessed is the man who finds wisdom and the man who gains understanding.

—Proverbs 3:13

If you ask people what it would take to make them happy, you will probably hear them say such things as more money, a bigger house, or a brand-new car. Some may say being able to work for themselves and not working for anyone else. Maybe a trip around the world or a new mate. Granted, these things may add to your happiness. True happiness, true wealth, however, you can only obtain through God's wisdom.

The biblical principle of obtaining true wealth demands that we honor God with the best that we have, from the beginning. Do not delay offering your first fruit to God, the very best of yourself. Not only does he desire the first portion of your wealth; he also desires to be the very first to be consulted in all of your plans. He wants to be first in your decisions, so do not make any without first consulting his will.

Before starting any business venture, first seek God's ultimate blueprint for success. Prior to making vows with your future mate, seek God's will with regard to the marriage. Marriage is about more than having someone to spend the rest of your life with; it is about giving birth to and raising up the next generation of people after God's own heart. Before making alliances with others, first go to God in prayer; he knows the intent of every man's heart, and he knows who is honest, as well as who is wicked and corrupt.

With the same wisdom, God created the heavens and the earth and everything on it. It is a waste of time trying to create a better format for acquiring happiness and wealth. Instead of spending countless hours trying to follow the way of the world and using their strategies for obtaining wealth, seek the wisdom of God and watch as the blessings of God overtake your life. Honor God with the best of yourself from the beginning. The result of such honor is satisfaction, prosperity, long life, happiness, riches, honor, delightful ways, and perfect peace.

Take the First Step

1. In what area of your life do you feel frustrated? Have you taken time to seek God's will concerning that situation?

_____

_____

_____

_____

_____

_____

_____

_____

2. Where do you need the wisdom of God right now?

_____

_____

_____

_____

_____

_____

_____

_____

3. Where can you find God's wisdom concerning your
    situation? (Hint: prayer, Bible, Christian counselor,
    faith-based books written by other Christians.)

_____

_____

_____

_____

_____

_____

_____

Focused Thought:

"Godly wisdom is the source of true, lasting happiness."

Carla's Coaching Challenge

In your quest to live the life of your dreams and find success
and fulfillment, seek first the wisdom of God concerning every
area of your life.

Journal Entry

Wait On

Then Naomi said, "Wait my daughter, until you find
out what happens. For the man will not rest until the
matter is settled today."

—Ruth 3:18

Patience truly is a virtue. One of the hardest things for people
to do is to wait. I have witnessed people get angry because they
had to wait in traffic or stand in line in the grocery store. I have
been guilty of getting a little agitated myself, especially after a
long, trying day at work.

When it comes to our dreams and desires, we give
ourselves permission to wait. That is, as long as we are simply
daydreaming. We give ourselves all the time we need. Until we
get enough money, enough education, until we are married, or
until someone gives us helping hand. I know many people who
are willing to put off their dreams until the kids are finished
college or even until retirement age. Once we have made up
our mind to pursue our dreams, however, waiting somehow
becomes one of the hardest things to do.

Sometimes we are even tempted to give up on our dreams
because we simply get tired of waiting and start to believe that
the vision will not manifest itself. It is during this time that

our imaginations begin to run wild. All of a sudden, all those outside negative forces begin to take root in our minds. Two of the main ones are fear and doubt.

When fear comes into our thoughts, we begin to doubt the dreams. We begin to doubt our ability to see things through to the end. Sometimes we may go as far as to say, "Who am I to believe that I have what it takes to accomplish something so great?" It is during this time that we begin to fear what others will say about us, especially if we fail to do what we said we could do. We begin to think about the people who told us that we did not have what it takes to accomplish our goals and dreams.

Perhaps what others will say may not even be an issue, but maybe it's what you feel they might do. Maybe you have put off your dreams, fearful that your spouse will leave you if you take time for yourself by pursuing your vision. Maybe you think that your kids will hold it against you if you dare insist that they clean up the dishes while you retreat to your new home office to research a subject matter that you are interested in pursuing. I am here to tell you that your dreams can come true, if you continue to believe. If you continue to have faith in God, yourself, and your vision, your dreams will come true at the appointed time.

If you simply dream and never take action toward creating the life you desire, nothing will happen. If you have put a plan in place and have taken the required action to make your dreams come true, however, then know that your vision will manifest itself.

Some things, like completing a task or multiple tasks, are within our control. We have no control, however, over other people or over fate. Some things simply require that we wait, and wait we must, if we desire to see our hard work and plans come to fruition.

Time is required for all things to fall into the proper order. Some people may say that it is a coincidence when you are in the right place at the right time. What they fail to realize, however, is that you have been working, waiting, and praying for the right moment and the prime opportunity for a breakthrough for quite a while.

Trust that God, who gave you the desires and dreams, the same God that blessed you with your talents, gifts, and abilities, is the same God who is in control of time. Therefore, I encourage you to wait. The vision will come to those who continue in faith. Many people start in a race strong, fast and determined to win. The one who gives up along the way because he had no staying power will not win. The one who endures to the end, however, will indeed meet with great success.

Take the First Step

1. Do you know exactly what it is that you desire to have in your life? What are you waiting on that requires patience?

_____

_____

_____

_____

_____

_____

_____

2. What action can you take toward your goals while you are waiting?

_____

_____

_____

_____

_____

_____

_____

_____

3. What can you do to rid yourself of despair, impatience, and doubt as you wait on the desires of your heart?

_____

_____

_____

_____

_____

_____

_____

Focused Thought:

"All things come to him who waits—provided he knows what he is waiting for."

—Woodrow Wilson

Carla's Coaching Challenge

The next time you feel like giving up on your dreams, just put them aside for a while and simply wait. Take time to pray and wait on God's timing.

Journal Entry

Live Your Dreams out Loud

> Wherefore the king said unto me, why is thy countenance
> sad, seeing thou art not sick? This is nothing else but
> sorrow of heart. Then I was very sore afraid.
>   —Nehemiah 2:2 (KJV)

In the above passage, Nehemiah became afraid because his
sad countenance could have been mistaken as mischief toward
the king. He could have lost his life just because of suspicion.
Nehemiah, however, believed in his vision. He had a vision for
restoration of the walls of Jerusalem. He had a deep desire to
leave his current position in order to fulfill his purpose, which
was to make a difference in the lives of others.

When was the last time someone noticed a change in your
countenance? Once we make a decision to pursue our vision
and dreams, we usually become excited and happy because we
have discovered our purpose and are ready to embark on a new
direction in life. We become joyful and ready to approach each
day with enthusiasm. The minute someone asks us about the
reason for such joy, however, we, too, become apprehensive. We
usually do not fear for our personal safety, but we are afraid of
others judging us, or we fear that someone will tell us that the
dream we have for our life is impossible.

I want to encourage you to live your dreams out loud. Do not be afraid to share your vision with others, especially if asked. You have spent countless hours praying, asking God to open doors of opportunity; you have done everything that you are supposed to do. No man, however, can succeed alone.

Open up and share your dream with others. You never know who will be able to give you an opportunity that will open many other doors for you. Start right now; speak your dream out loud, right where you are. Tell the next person you see about your dreams. Do not worry about how or when this dream will come about. Make a commitment to live your dream out loud.

Take the First Step

1. Who can you get as an accountability partner—someone who believes in you and your abilities? Tell him or her about your dream as often as necessary so that you can keep your dream alive. This person can be a close friend, spouse, mentor, or life coach.

_____

_____

_____

_____

_____

_____

_____

_____

2. Set a goal to reach your dreams. Setting SMART goals (specific, measurable, attainable, realistic, and timely) will ensure that you reach your goals in less time.

_____

_____

_____

_____

_____

_____

_____

_____

_____

3. Create a vision board for your dream. Cut out pictures and words that will inspire you and keep your vision before you on a daily basis.

_____

_____

_____

_____

_____

_____

_____

_____

Focused Thought:
"Do not fear how others will perceive your dreams."

Carla's Coaching Challenge

Be prepared to tell someone what you desire at a moment's notice. You never know how they may be able to assist you in making your dream come true.

Journal Entry

_____

_____

_____

_____

_____

_____

_____

_____

_____

_____

_____

_____

_____

_____

_____

_____

_____

_____

_____

_____

_____

_____

_____

_____

_____

_____

Big is Just an Illusion

And David said to Saul, Let no man's heart fail because
of him.

1 Samuel 17:32 (KJV)

Many people put off pursuing their desires and dreams because
of fear and doubt. They struggle with an earnest desire to
accomplish something great in their lives only to put off their
decision for months or even years because of a perceived
obstacle. In the noted scripture, David is saying, "Do not give
up on your dream because the illusion of a giant is standing in
your way."

What is stopping you from living the life of your dreams?
Have you come up against any giants in your path to living
the life you desire? Perhaps you desire to attend college, start
a business of your own, purchase your dream home, lose ten
pounds, get married to your dream person, or run a marathon.
What obstacles have presented themselves as a giant—
something to fear or hold you back? What obstacle has caused
you to lose heart and give up on your most treasured dream?

One of the strategies that David used to overcome his
fear was to find out what the reward was for killing the giant.
He found out that the king offered great riches and the hand

of his daughter in marriage to the person who succeeded in eliminating the giant.

Think about your dreams. What reward will you receive if you overcame your obstacles? If you decide to apply for a position that requires you to overcome your fear of rejection, just remember the reward of a higher salary, a new house, or an increase in savings. Once you begin to realign your focus on the reward, your obstacle will become something you will more likely be willing to overcome because your reward will be bigger than the obstacle.

Another strategy that David used was to consider his unique abilities, talents, and gifts. His gifts were the very things that benefited him at a challenging time in his life. He was not comfortable coveting someone else's gifts or talents, but relied on the very parts of himself that had been of use to him in dealing with other challenges in his life. How have you overcome other obstacles in your life? What tactics did you use?

I remember the day that I decided that I wanted to take steps to purchase my first home. I had always dreamed of owning my own home, but I believed at the time that it was beyond my reach (giant). On this particular day, I was attending a co-worker's housewarming celebration. My heart began to speak to me, saying, "Wait a minute, you hold the same position on your job that this person does, you earn about the same salary, and you have good credit. If it is possible for her, why not you?"

I later spoke to with my co-worker about the steps that she had taken to achieve her dream of home ownership. She happily explained what she had done, referred me to her real estate agent, and wished me well. She encouraged me to go for it.

Once I called the agent, she explained to me that I would need a down payment, at which point my heart attempted to fail me. I earned a decent salary, but I had never really saved any significant amount of money. The agent explained to me that it would take about three months from that day to close on a property. My biggest dream at that time was to own a home of my own (reward). My biggest obstacle was the down payment that I had to obtain (giant).

My plan was to work with what I had. I knew how to live without luxuries, so I gave up spending, except for necessities, and started saving every spare dollar that I earned. I knew how to work hard, so I got a part-time job. I knew how to rely on God for strength, so I would work thirteen days straight, including a double shift on Saturdays, and attend church every other Sunday. I kept to this schedule for three months.

Whenever I found myself extremely tired, I would ask God to restore my strength. When my feet ached halfway through my second shift on Saturday, I would sometimes cry and ask God to see me through another day. Whenever I was tempted to spend money, which was not often, because I was always so tired, I would envision the rooms in my new home. Seeing them decorated to my liking gave me the desire to stick to my plans.

When the three months were up, I had earned enough for the down payment with money to spare. After closing on my house, I immediately put the key in the door and spent a few minutes walking through my new home, giving God all the praise. Afterward I was able to take some of the extra money to the furniture store to purchase new furnishings for my home.

Coming up with a down payment for my home appeared to me a giant obstacle until I developed a plan. What appeared to be a giant was simply an illusion. Once I put my plan in place, I began implementing the steps by using my God-given talents, gifts, and abilities, also trusting that the same God who had helped me overcome other obstacles in my life would be there to assist me in overcoming this, too.

Take the First Step

1. A. List your No. 1 goal.

_____

_____

_____

_____

_____

B. List the obstacle that stands in the way of your achieving your goal.

_____

_____

_____

_____

C. List the reward of overcoming the obstacles listed above.

_____

_____

_____

_____

_____

2. List the talents, gifts, and unique abilities that have helped you to achieve your goals in the past.

_____

_____

_____

_____

_____

_____

_____

3. Write down three actions that you can implement immediately to begin fulfilling your dream.

_____

_____

_____

_____

_____

_____

_____

_____

Focused Thought:

"Your problem is only as big as you allow it to be."

Carla's Coaching Challenge

Start working on your goals today.

Journal Entry

The Way Is Made Known

Trust in the LORD with all thine heart and lean not on your own understanding; in all your ways acknowledge him, and he will make your paths straight.

Proverbs 3:5–6

For most of my life, I have been sure of only one thing and that is that God is always with me. He has always been there, through the good times and the difficult times. This knowing is my secret to believing that I will always find the way to whatever or wherever it is that I am seeking. As far back as I can remember, I have never been a person to think that I cannot accomplish something. I may have said it, but, deep within me, I never meant it. There is an old saying that goes, "Where there is a will, there is a way." My personal saying is, "Acknowledge God in every situation in your life, and you will know the way."

Many people begin to seek out God during times of turmoil and distress—when life seems unbearable or when a situation appears to be impossible. During times of creativity and expansion, however, I have witnessed myself and others get so overwhelmed and excited about the great things happening in our lives that we edge God out of the whole process.

Many people truly believe that it is only okay to ask God to help them overcome bad situations such as illness, loss of a home, or a defiant child. I have noticed, however, that when I suggest to some people that they should also seek God for the desires of their heart concerning abundance and prosperity, they immediately shut down. Some people believe that it is a selfish act. Jesus states in the book of John, however, "I am come that they may have life and that they may have *it* more abundantly." (KJV)

God is there with you even through the joys of your life. He desires to show you the way to abundance and creativity. As you seek to create the life of your dreams, take time to acknowledge him. If you desire to purchase your dream home and you are currently struggling with your finances, do not immediately say "It is impossible" or "It is just a dream"; acknowledge him in your dreams and desires. Instead of immediately saying, "I can't" to your dreams and desires, say "God show me how to make my dreams come true." A light is less noticeable during the day, when the sun is shining brightly and excitement is all around; nevertheless, it continues to shine.

This morning, around six o'clock, I had a desire to write a chapter of this book. I began to have self-doubts, saying to myself, *Your writing is not good enough.* I did not immediately respond by agreeing that I cannot write; instead I acknowledged the will of God concerning my purpose for writing this book. Once again, the words began to flow as I pulled out a sheet of paper and a pen and trusted God to allow the words to appear.

When was the last time you acknowledged God in your desires and dreams? Do you believe that he desires you to have a life overflowing with love, joy, peace, excitement, creativity, friends, family, wealth, success, the abundance of life? Allow God to direct your path in living your dreams. Do not spend so much time figuring out how. Take time to ask him to show you the way. With God, all things really are possible.

For some of you, success could mean overcoming a negative behavior, an addiction, restoring your self-esteem, becoming more assertive, or prioritizing your life. Perhaps it is choosing to live a lifestyle that is congruent with your true values, or simply living a balanced lifestyle, creating a budget for your household finances, putting your family first, or living a healthier lifestyle. Trust that God is with you and desires to show you the way.

Take the First Step

1. List five things that are challenging to you in your life.

_____

_____

_____

_____

_____

_____

_____

2. Say a simple prayer acknowledging the power of God and his ability to help you every situation of your life.

_____

_____

_____

_____

_____

_____

_____

3. After you have prayed, sit quietly and listen to the voice of your spirit. Take a moment to write out any suggestions that you receive.

_____

_____

_____

_____

_____

_____

_____

_____

Focused Thought:

"Allow God to lead you as you pursue your dreams and desires, and he will walk before you, removing all obstacles from your path."

Carla's Coaching Challenge

Take that concern or problem that you have and commit it to God so that you can gain a new perspective about your situation.

Journal Entry

The Other Side of the Storm

He said to his disciples, "Let us go over to the other side."

Mark 4:35

The trials and tribulations we experience as we seek to fulfill our purpose, we at times refer to as the storms in our lives. By storms, I mean elements in life that tear down, destroy, and defeat. There is a deeper, more meaningful purpose to a storm, however. You must come to a place of understanding about the true purpose of a storm. It would also behoove you to develop insight about the higher good that you are to achieve along those stormy journeys.

A storm is a key element to success in life. It is a key element to making it to the other side of our trials and struggles. In the Bible, the book of Hebrews speaks of God "once again shaking the earth, which signifies the removal of what can be shaken, so that what cannot be shaken can remain." Only the strong can survive the storms of life.

I once heard someone say, "A strong wind will cause apples to fall from a tree, but upon further inspection you will notice that the ones that have fallen are rotten and invaded with worms. The ones that remain on the tree are the good apples." All the good apples remain on the tree waiting for harvest, and to be used for their true purpose.

In the above passage, Jesus states, "Let us go to the other side." The disciple's purpose was established. Jesus was with them all throughout their journey. Like any great teacher, he left them alone to put to the test all that they had learned from him. He had taught them many lessons about speaking to their mountains (obstacles), having faith, even as small as mustard seeds. "How is it that you have not faith?" asks Jesus—not only in his ability to save them, but faith in the ability he had given them to save themselves.

Why continue to struggle against the storms in your life when God has equipped you with such great gifts, talents, and abilities? He has given spiritual qualities to those who have walked side by side with him in prayer, devotion, and meditation. God has equipped you as leaders to speak to the storms in your life.

Troubled waters teach us that we cannot succeed on our own. Just when we begin to believe we have achieved a measure of success and that life will be smooth sailing all the way, a storm will come our way—not to discourage or stop us, but to humble us, so that we must yield ourselves and live in total dependence on the power of God.

When the storms of life come your way, you will lose all sense of direction; you will no longer have control of the strong winds or the course that you will travel. A storm will make your formal training appear null and void. At that time, you must come to realize that it is the will and power of God that will get you to the other side of the storm.

I remember a very challenging time in my life, a time when I thought that I was in total control. My career was on track; I held a management position in a job that I loved. I was earning a salary that far exceeded any amount that I could have imagined at the time. I had returned to college to further my education, purchased my second home, and had recently gotten married.

I was a licensed minister, teaching and encouraging others the wisdom of God's word; my life was perfect.

It was right around this time of my life that a strong wind began to blow. A storm was brewing in my life. Life as I thought it was to be began to shatter right before my eyes. I lost my job, and, at the same time, I faced a challenging illness that took all my energy and strength. I was no longer able to keep up with my current budget, which meant financial struggles. This all happened around the same time that I was to complete the final courses toward my degree. I was unable to keep up, so I failed my courses and could not graduate. Did I mention that I had recently gotten married?

I certainly was not, at that time in my life, the easiest person to live with. I believe I was born with an independent spirit. I had always had the natural ability to pick up my bed and walk with it. This time, however, was different. I was no longer in control.

I had finally come to a place where I found that the only logical choice that I could make was to surrender. My life was not my own. My life was in the hands of God. That was the day that a little light began to shine, and God was able to direct my life toward the other side of the storm. It was not easy, but it was worth it. My life took on a new meaning. I no longer wanted to succeed at obtaining things but desired to succeed at fulfilling my purpose in life, finding the meaning of true success and inspiring others to do the same.

Are you currently facing any storms in your life? Have you had to deal with any life-altering situation in your life that left you feeling helpless and unequipped? I would like to encourage you by telling you that you, too, can weather the storms in your life. You, too, can stand against the storms of life that come your way. That is, if you are willing to stop and realize that God is on board with you, traveling with you to the other side.

Surrender all your plans to his perfect will for your life, and you will find that you can make it safely to the other side of the storm. Not only will you be stronger and wiser; you will also emerge with a great sense of purpose and passion for life.

Take the First Step

1. List any major challenges that you are currently facing in your life.

_____

_____

_____

_____

_____

_____

_____

2. What plans do you feel you need surrender to God?

_____

_____

_____

_____

_____

_____

_____

3. A storm will sometimes reveal things that are not beneficial for your life. What behavior, people, or things do you feel God is trying to remove from your life?

_____

_____

_____

_____

_____

_____

_____

_____

Focused Thought:

"When you find yourself in the middle of a storm, remember that you are not alone."

Carla's Coaching Challenge

Whenever you are facing challenging situations in your life and feel that you have lost total control, simply surrender. Use this time to reflect, to commune with the spirit within you. Sometimes these storms in our lives are necessary to get our attention so that we can move onto the path that leads to our true purpose.

Journal Entry

Yes, You Really Can

"I can do all things through Christ which strengtheneth me."

Philippians 4:13 (KJV)

I often think back over the days in my life when it was a constant struggle just to make it to the next day. There were many times when I was unsure whether I even wanted to make it. When I think back over the first three and a half decades of my life, I often refer to them as my survival days.

I call those days my survival days because during those times there was a constant struggle in my inner being. I struggled to know who I really was. I struggled to believe that I had any real value in my life. I struggled with the idea that I was unworthy of anything or anybody. I struggled with the issue of forgiving others and forgiving myself. I struggled with thoughts that no one had ever really loved me just for being me.

I call those days survival days because it appeared that it was always me against the whole world. It was always me with my screwed up thoughts. It was as if I spent my days living in a wilderness, trying to decide which way would lead to a place of freedom and peace. Survival was about always walking a new and different path, always making decisions out of fear, doubt, loneliness, self-pity, sadness, and pain.

I call those days survival because, at any given moment, I had to decide whether I would continue on a journey that offered little promise of a new life or give in to that little voice in my head. It would say, "If you gave up on life, no one would care if you drove your car off the road, over a steep hill, and your pain and sorrow would be over." I call those days survival because each day I had to find strength to make it through yet another day.

Finding strength would have been too much for me, with the state of mind that I was in those days. The good news is that strength just showed up whenever I needed it. It was there the night that I cried because I was fatherless and needed a father's comfort. I heard a voice that said, "I am your father."

Strength was there the night that I needed a reason to live, a reason more powerful than the pain that was in my heart. I heard a voice that said, "Work with my children." As strange as those words may seem, they were the very words that gave me a reason to keep living. These words let me know that one day everything would make sense and that I had a purpose for my life.

Strength was there to speak firmly to me in the wee hours of one particular morning to say, "No more" to self-defeating behaviors and habits. Strength would always show up when it appeared that I needed it most, through all the pain, struggles, defeats, disappointments, failures, and losses. As I was led by strength out of the wilderness, into a land of promise, a land of provision, happiness, extreme joy, love, and passion—a place of light, abundance, forgiveness, and peace—I have come to realize that strength is still with me.

`The same strength that held my hand, protected my heart, made ways of provision in my time of survival is the same strength that is with me in my time of abundance, creativity, and newness of life. If I was able to endure, with the strength of God, during my days of survival, how much more will I be able to live and prosper by this same strength?

You, too, can do all things through Christ, who strengthens you. You must understand that the same God that gives you strength through hard times in your life is also there to strengthen you during your times of creativity and abundance of life.

I want to encourage you to know that, yes, you really can live the life of your dreams. Yes, you really can fulfill your life's purpose. Yes, you really can live a life of abundance, passion, joy, peace, and excitement. With God, all things really are possible. You can do all that you desire through Christ, who strengthens you with love, talents, gift, abilities, and creative power.

Take the First Step

1. Start a gratitude journal. Begin by listing all the times in your life that you were able to overcome adversity with the help of strength greater than your own.

_____

_____

_____

_____

_____

_____

_____

2. Journal about your desires, your dreams, and your purpose in life.

_____
_____
_____
_____
_____
_____
_____
_____

3. Take time to say a prayer of thanks for help in your times of struggles and your times of creativity and abundance.

_____
_____
_____
_____
_____
_____
_____
_____

Focused Thought:

"Yes, You Really Can live the life of *your* dreams."

Carla's Coaching Challenge

Go for it. Start dreaming; believe in what appears to be impossible. Take the first step to creating and living the life of your dreams. Get a mentor, a life coach—someone who believes in you and will hold you accountable for reaching your goals. Remember, **it is possible**. You have what it takes to succeed in life. You have a divine purpose to fulfill. You will find yourself living a more fulfilling and successful life.

Journal Entry

Do Something

Whatever he does prospers.

—Psalm 1:3

Have you ever had a gut feeling that you were supposed to accomplish something great? As a young girl, around the age of eleven or twelve, I carried around this strong feeling that I had great purpose to fulfill. Something deep within me sensed that one day, when I grew up, I would be a part of something much bigger than I could ever imagine. The problem was that I grew up, yet still I found myself waiting for something great to happen in my life.

Like many other faithful believers in God, I was waiting for him to do something extremely miraculous that would cause this big thing to come about. I would often feel that maybe it did not happen because I was not being nice enough or maybe I had to remove some type of God-forbidden behavior from my life.

I would often feel that if I just spent more time reading the Bible, praying, or fasting, my blessing would come. Then I would begin to think things were not happening for me because I needed to attend church even more than I already was. Maybe I needed to volunteer more, become a better person, a better wife, daughter, sister, and friend.

One day as I grew in my understanding of God, I began to see that it was simply God's will that each of his children accomplish great things. Without doubt, his desire is that we are genuinely good people and give of ourselves to help others. The desire to achieve something great, however, originated from God's divine plan for me to have abundance, to prosper, and do great exploits.

It finally dawned on me that while I was waiting on God to do something great for me, he was trying to tell me all along that the secret to greatness lies in what I decided to do for myself. God had already laid the groundwork for me to prosper. There was no more for him to do except to share his knowledge, wisdom, and understanding as I began to take hold of my God-inspired desires, talents, and abilities. I simply had to do something with them in order to receive all that he desired for me to have, knowing that, whatever I chose to do with my life, God would cause me to prosper.

Prosperity is not something that just falls from the sky like rain or snow. Prosperity is the result of something that you purposely do. If you desire to prosper in health, you must exercise, eat right, and take good care of your physical body. If you desire to prosper financially, you must give, save, make wise investments, and become a good steward over your money—and work smart.

If you desire to be successful in your business or career, you must understand your strengths and weaknesses, your unique gifts, talents, and abilities. You must also use them to do something that you feel God has equipped you to do.

If you have a beautiful voice and a desire to sing, then sing. If you can swim well, do that, or maybe teach others. If you have a love of knowledge, learn all you can on a subject or two, become an expert, and teach others. If you have a passion for writing, write books or poems.

Maybe you have a heart of great compassion and love to give to others; then consider starting a nonprofit organization, learn about grants that are available, and start giving immediately. If you have a tendency to be a little bossy, and enjoy showing others what to do, understand that these are not weaknesses, but strengths. Use them wisely. Take classes in leadership, get a higher education, and start seeking positions that require you to lead an organization or movement.

If you have a special love for children, consider taking a few courses in childcare; apply for licensing as a provider so you can start your own day care. If you enjoy working with your hands, learn a skill and start your own business fixing or building something. Just do something because God wants you to prosper.

Once you have done all that you are able to do with all the knowledge, wisdom, gifts, talents, and abilities with which God has equipped you, then God has an instrument to use to pour out his many blessings to you.

What is it that you desire to do? What is it specifically that you want from God? Do not just sit around with an empty bucket waiting for God to fill it. Leave the bucket where it is and get busy doing something toward living your dreams and fulfilling your desires. One day in the future, you will notice that not only did God fill that empty bucket with multiples gifts, talents skills, and resources; you will also find that he multiplied them beyond your greatest belief.

Take the First Step

1. Name one step you can take today toward living the life of your dreams.

    _____

    _____

    _____

    _____

    _____

    _____

    _____

2. Write the name of one or two people who you can contact today to assist you with getting started.

    _____

    _____

    _____

    _____

    _____

    _____

    _____

3. Write a statement of affirmation about your commitment.

    _____

    _____

    _____

    _____

    _____

    _____

    _____

Focused Thought:

"Nothing happens until you do something."

Carla's Coaching Challenge

Make a commitment today to take action concerning your dreams. I desire that you prosper, but most of all it is God's desire to see you prosper in all that you do. Get busy; take the first step to living the life your dreams.

Journal Entry

About the Author

Having the desire to persevere and live the life of your dreams in spite of life's challenges takes courage and an unstoppable mind-set. As a born dreamer, Carla was astonished to look back over her life and realize that she was not even close to living the life she had always imagined for herself. After resolving to discover what was hindering her from living the life of her God-inspired dreams, Carla sought God for her life's purpose. Once she was sure of God's will for her life, she wrote out a strategic plan to put her back on the path of her desired life.

Carla has a passion for inspiring others to live their God-inspired dreams by taking the necessary steps to overcome their fears, doubts, and self-limiting beliefs.

Carla is much more than a survivor herself; she has a heart of compassion for others who are facing many of life's challenges. As a healthcare worker for the past several years, she has witnessed many people who face physical and health challenges and find it difficult to see past their current situation. Carla has developed a commitment to encouraging others to embrace life, to overcome obstacles, and step beyond boundaries.

As a disciple of Christ, she has observed as negative thoughts and beliefs have infiltrated the minds of God's children and have discouraged them from believing in what is possible for their lives. She desires to show others that with God all things really are possible.

Carla Burrows is founder and CEO of Empowered Living, LLC, a personal development company with a mission to ignite hope and possibility in the lives of women.

As an author, life coach, and speaker, Carla enjoys working with women who desires to succeed in life, but lack the hope and belief in themselves to meet the challenge. She provides insightful tools and information that empower, inspire, and teach women to overcome fears, doubts, and self-limiting beliefs that hold them back from living the life they deserve and desire.

She is a contributing author of "The Woman's Handbook For Self-Confidence," a certified seminar trainer in Women's Issues and a certified life coach.

Carla resides in Chesterfield, Virginia, with her husband, Terry. She is available for speaking, life coaching, and seminars.

For More Information

For a **free subscription** to Carla's newsletter, "Empowering Secrets of Successful Women", and other valuable resources, or for complete information on booking Carla to speak for your association or group, contact her through www.carlaburrows. com.